THE

SEVEN

LAST

WORDS

OF

JESUS

Alfred McBride, O. Praem.

The Seven Last Words of Jesus

 St. Anthony Messenger Press
CINCINNATI, OHIO

Nihil Obstat: Rev. Lawrence Landini, O.F.M.
Rev. Christopher R. Armstrong

Imprimi Potest: Rev. John Bok, O.F.M.
Provincial

Imprimatur: +James H. Garland, V.G.
Archdiocese of Cincinnati
July 2, 1990

Scripture citations are taken from *The New American Bible With Revised New Testament,* copyright ©1986 by the Confraternity of Christian Doctrine, and are used by permission. All rights reserved. Material from *Converts, Dropouts, Returnees: A Study of Religious Change Among Catholics,* written by Dean R. Hoge with Kenneth McGuire, C.S.P., and Bernard F. Stratman, S.M., copyright ©1981 United States Catholic Conference, published by United States Catholic Conference, is used with permission. The passage from *The Calvary Christ* by Gerald O'Collins, S.J., copyright ©1977 by SCM Press Ltd., is used by permission of Westminster/John Knox Press. The excerpt from *The Religions of Man* by Huston Smith, copyright ©1958 by Huston Smith, is used by permission of Harper & Row, Publishers, Inc. The passage from *Seven Pillars of Wisdom* by T. E. Lawrence, copyright ©1938 Garden Publishing Company, is used by permission of Doubleday, a division of Bantam, Doubleday, Dell Publishing Group, Inc. The passage from *Poems of Dylan Thomas,* copyright ©1952 by Dylan Thomas, is reprinted by permission of New Directions Publishing Corp. The passage from "The Gay Science," from *The Portable Nietzsche,* translated by Walter Kaufmann, copyright ©1954 by The Viking Press, Inc., copyright © renewed 1982 by Viking Penguin, Inc., is reprinted by permission of Viking Penguin, a division of Penguin Books USA, Inc. Used with permission are excerpts from the English translation of *Rite of Holy Week* ©1972, International Committee on English in the Liturgy, Inc. All rights reserved. The excerpt from *Journeys to Glory: A Celebration of the Human Spirit,* by Adam Bujack (photographs) and Marjorie B. Young (text), copyright ©1976 by Marjorie B. Young, is used by permission of HarperCollins Publishers Inc. The passage from Dietrich Bonhoeffer's *Letters and Papers from Prison,* revised, enlarged edition, copyright ©1953, 1967, 1971 by SCM Press, Ltd., is used by permission of Macmillan Publishing Company.

Cover and book design by Julie Lonneman

ISBN 0-86716-149-3

©1990, Alfred McBride
All rights reserved.

Published by St. Anthony Messenger Press
Printed in the U.S.A.

ACKNOWLEDGEMENTS

The meditations in this book developed from a series of sermons on the Seven Last Words, first given at St. John the Evangelist Church in New York City on Good Friday, 1989. I am grateful to the pastor, Monsignor Michael Wrenn, and his parishioners for that opportunity. I also thank Monsignor George Bardes and the parishioners of St. Thomas More Parish, New York City, where the sermons were given again in 1990. Lastly, I thank Carol Luebering, my editor, whose wise guidance in this and three other of my books has kept me firm in my purpose and disciplined in my expression.

Contents

The Song of the Thorn Bird

A ccording to legend, the thorn bird sings just once in its life. Leaving its nest, it searches for a bush with long, sharp thorns. Upon finding such a bush it impales itself on the biggest thorn. At that moment it begins to sing. The bird outcarols the lark and the nightingale and the world pauses to listen. God smiles with pleasure at the captivating melody. What is the message of this sacrificial music? Life's most satisfying moment can be purchased only at the price of great pain—so says the legend.

The seven last words of Jesus are like the song of the thorn bird. The Word of God left the "nest" of divine love and glory and communion to become incarnate in Jesus Christ; the Logos made an act of sacrificial love intended to draw all people back into harmony with God. In the first Sermon on the Mount Jesus outlined the attitudes that would make reconciliation with God and one another possible. Impaled on the thorn of the cross, Jesus acted out his teachings. His last words constitute a song of love as well as an act of redemption.

To speak of the seven words as a song is not to say they are just music meant to enchant, entertain or soothe the soul. In true biblical style, Christ's final words are deeds. He had preached forgiveness on the mount overlooking the sea of Galilee. At Calvary his word of forgiveness was an action. His paradise promise to the repentant thief was an act of salvation. His word to Mary and John accomplished her future security as well as her new role as Mother of the Church. His word of surrender to his Father was the active gathering of his whole being toward God.

The biblical word—in Hebrew, *dabar*—was considered to have power. Talk is not cheap in Scripture. Biblical people believed the word was the creative force bringing the world into existence. In their oral culture (where language was no idle matter) they also thought that their own words possessed the force of blessing and cursing.

Oral cultures take the word seriously. In our own document-oriented culture the written word clearly has force. Lawyers are fond of tracking down the "paper trail" in support of their cases. In Scripture, on the other hand, the spoken word has a life of its own. It is an active force that, once released, accomplishes what it says. The power of a name was well known. That is why the wrong use of God's name was thought to be so destructive.

Christ spoke his seven last words in a biblical culture that attributed the force of action to his utterances. Passivity did not mark the time Jesus spent on the cross. He composed a love song in seven parts. He wove the melody of his words into the perfect unity of his sufferings for our salvation. Far from being self-absorbed in his pain, Jesus provided his own commentary on the meaning of what he was doing—indeed, even making the comments saving acts themselves. By word, example and action Jesus gave us a lesson in the art of dying. He also showed how the process of dying could be redemptive. Now our own inevitable rendezvous with death can be accomplished with similar dignity and with saving power both for ourselves and for all our sisters and brothers.

The seven last words are scattered through the Gospels:

1) Father, forgive them, they know not what they do (Luke 23:34a).

2) Amen, I say to you, today you will be with me in Paradise (Luke 23:43b).

3) [He] said to his mother, "Woman, behold, your son." Then he said to the disciple, "Behold, your mother" (John 19:26b-27a).

4) My God, my God, why have you forsaken me? (Matthew 27:46b; Mark 15:34b).

5) I thirst (John 19:28b).

6) It is finished (John 19:30b).

7) Father, into your hands I commend my spirit (Luke 23:46b).

They are ordered by pious tradition, not by strict historical chronology. Luke and John differ on Jesus' final utterance due to the traditions and purposes of each writer. The liturgical tradition reflected in John favored making Christ's ritual word his last one. The prayer motif in Luke suited the use of Christ's devotional farewell as the ultimate word. The tradition of the devotion chooses the Lucan word as the last one.

Scripture scholars say that the first part of the gospel to be preached was the passion and resurrection of Christ. This is the core message of Christianity. In the following meditations we reflect once again on the passion as seen and heard through our Lord's seven last words.

The Last Temptation

Father, forgive them, they know not what they do. LUKE 23:34a

The Persians invented crucifixion. The Romans adopted it for the execution of non-Roman criminals, especially murderers and robbers.

A trumpeter led the crucifixion procession to the execution mound. The music both drew a crowd and admonished people to get out of the way of the procession. Behind the trumpeter came a herald who carried a wooden poster bearing the name of the criminal and identifying the crime. This created the possibility, according to ancient custom, of having a second trial on the spot. Someone could propose new evidence and ask that the criminal be retried. An official from the court would oversee a hearing. If the new evidence proved innocence, the criminal would be released.

The criminal walked behind the herald, carrying the T-bar of the cross. The vertical post stood at the mound of execution. Four guards marched with the criminal. A centurion, usually mounted on a horse, came last.

The Setting

The site of Christ's crucifixion was just a short distance outside the walls of Jerusalem. Scripture calls it Golgotha, "the place of the skull" (see Matthew 27:33). The Latin for *Golgotha* is *Calvarium*, Calvary. Some think that it is called

"Skull Hill" because it used to be a place for beheading. A legend claims that the skull of Adam was buried there. (The Chapel of Adam in the Church of the Holy Sepulcher in Jerusalem derives its name from this legend.) The imagination of its unknown author portrayed the blood of Christ flowing down upon Adam's skull. Though the legend is false, its message remains true, namely, that the blood of Christ, the new Adam, redeemed the original Adam.

Countless artistic depictions of the crucifixion portray the mound as a small mountain and the post of the cross as a soaring, vertical tree. The reality was much simpler. The mound was little more than a small rise of packed earth; anchored in it was a post probably not more than 10 feet high. The victim would be close to both friends and enemies, easily able to conduct conversations with those nearby. Diaries and journals about crucifixions report that victims often lived as much as a week on their crosses and conversed with those who came to see them.

Crucifixion was a cruel form of execution—only being burned alive was deemed more painful by some—and it was a complicated, harsh and dirty method. The executioners tied the victim's wrists to the T-bar to minimize movement when the nails were driven into the wrist bone (not into the palms of the hands, which would be unable to sustain the weight of the body). Though recent research claims the shroud of Turin does not date from the time of Christ, it does show nails in the wrist bones of the crucified victim whose image it bears.

They mounted the body on the vertical post and nailed the feet to it. Further support was required to hold up the body, so a piece of wood was placed between the victim's legs. The Church Fathers symbolically compared this "seat" to Christ's throne of judgment and his chair of teaching. Very likely there was also a footrest for additional support. Confirmation for this may be seen in a third century pagan cartoon, meant to mock Christians, that shows the figure of the crucified Christ with a donkey's head and with his feet resting on a footboard.

Despite the pain and shock to the system caused by the nails, the victim rarely died from those wounds. Prior scourgings and beatings also caused blood loss and dehydration and general trauma. But one could survive all this. The real problem for the crucified was breathing. Increasing fatigue plus the pain involved in pulling oneself up to fill the lungs with fresh air meant that the victim died of gradual asphyxiation.

The Romans regularly executed their victims in the nude, but they made an exception for the Jews out of deference for their sense of modesty. Hence they placed a cloth around the loins of Christ.

The herald planted the wooden poster above the head of Jesus. Our crucifixes summarize its message with the acronym *INRI*, the initial letters of the Latin words that mean "Jesus Christ, King of the Jews." The original poster contained the message in Latin and Hebrew—the languages of the Roman officials and the people of Palestine—and in the Greek which was common to both and enabled the Romans and the Jews to communicate with each other.

The poster displayed the legal cause for execution. In this case, Jesus had sought unlawful and rebellious political power in the eyes of the Roman state. From the point of view of faith, it is also a proclamation of Jesus' royal messiahship, unwittingly announced by the representative of the world's greatest political power.

This was the physical setting for the last seven utterances of Jesus. He used the concluding moments of his life to deliver a few brief statements that in their simplicity create an environment of faith, hope and love amid what was otherwise a scene of horror, brutality and human perverseness at its worst.

Jesus Hears Challenges

The provocation for his first word came from what Jesus heard from those nearby. Scripture reports four challenges, all of which taunted him to save himself. The challengers all used the same Greek word for "save." They reminded Jesus of his reputation as a miracle worker. They tempted him to use power to solve his problem. To them the love of power solved most difficulties. They never understood his teaching that the power of love surpassed all other methods of healing personal tragedy and intractable human behavior.

Who were the challengers and what did they say?

1) *Religious leaders*—priests, scribes and elders—mocked Jesus about being a presumed savior. "[L]et him save himself if he is the chosen one, the Messiah of God" (Luke 23:35b). "Let him come down from the cross now, and we will believe in him" (Matthew 27:42b).

   These religious leaders believed they possessed the power of discerning who was truly the Messiah. Custodians of religious tradition, they assumed they were best equipped to identify the Messiah and the appearance of the Kingdom of God. They have assured themselves that Jesus is not the Messiah. Cynically, they mock the possibility of Jesus being the expected one and use that against him.

2) The *soldiers* jeered at him. "As they approached to offer him wine they called out, 'If you are King of the Jews, save yourself' " (Luke 23:36b-37).

   The soldiers are political-minded and in the service of an emperor. They know and admire the uses of power. They basically say, "If you are a politician, save yourself. Is not that the sign of a skilled politician?" Real kings do not let themselves be pushed around.

3) The *crowd* who came to watch the event taunted him about saying that he could destroy the temple and rebuild it in three days. "[I]f you are the Son of God,...come down from the cross!" (Matthew 27:40b).

   The crowd reflects a form of popular religion that looks for signs and wonders. Jesus had said that only an evil and adulterous generation looks for such things. That group now stands at the cross and watches him. They use the title *Son of God* to corner him. He should be able to come down from the cross if he, as God's Son, is able to tear down a temple and rebuild it.

4) *One of the robbers* hanging next to Jesus reviled him. "Are you not the Messiah? Save yourself and us" (Luke 23:39b). The robber repeats the accusation of the religious rulers.

The four challengers base their tests on the three main titles of Jesus: "If you are the *Messiah*" (religious leaders and the robber), "if you are a *king*" (soldiers), "if you are the *Son of God*" (crowd), "save yourself! Come down from the cross!"

The first temptation of Christ occurred during his 40 days of fasting and prayer in the desert, just prior to the beginning of his public ministry. Satan tempted him three times to look out for his own self-interest, to save himself from hunger, from the bother of inviting people to faith by loving witness, from the anonymity of being a powerless person in a provincial backwater.

The triple temptation at the beginning of Christ's ministry is repeated in the final hours of his earthly mission. Through the voices of the religious leaders, the robber, the crowd and the soldiers, Satan once again tempts Jesus to forget his true mission and to look out for himself. The message is, "Save yourself. Don't bother about saving the world."

> If you are the Son of God, command this stone to become bread. (Luke 4:3)

> [I]f you are the Son of God,...come down from the cross! (Matthew 27:40b)

Temptation From a Different Angle

The film *The Last Temptation of Christ*, based on the novel by Nikos Kazantzakis, approaches the scene at Calvary with the same view. There too Jesus is tempted to save himself and not the world. The angle of the temptation, however, is uniquely contemporary. The tempters in the Gospels begin with power images: Messiah, Son of God, King. The mood is mean-spirited and cruel. The tone of the challengers is one of disbelief even with the insistent request for a miracle.

The tempter in the film is a sweetly innocent little girl. She does not appeal to Jesus' majestic power to sweep aside his enemies, rather she awakens his awareness of his sexual urges and stimulates a fantasy about marrying Mary Magdalene and raising a family. The tempter diverts attention from spiritual—yes, divine—strengths and plays upon the human drive to be a husband and a father.

No miracle is expected or asked for. The challenge might be stated this way: "If you would like to get married and have a family, come down from the cross. Ask for a hearing. Apologize to the religious and political leaders and promise you will never bother them again."

As the 30-minute fantasy sequence unfolds, Jesus imagines himself marrying Mary Magdalene, having an adulterous relationship with Martha, raising a family and eventually confronting St. Paul with the "fact" that he never did die or rise from the dead. He hears Paul saying that doesn't matter, for Christianity's "lie" is more important for people's needs than Christ's "truth."

The fantasy ends with Jesus being visited on his deathbed by some apostles, who accuse him of betraying them and his mission. This causes his conversion and he comes out of his fantasy back to the cross, where he decides to go ahead with the crucifixion.

The film's 30-minute fantasy is preceded by a two-and-a-quarter-hour portrayal of Jesus as a laid-back and aimless man. Jesus comes across as a limpid, Western secular man, a male who has no backbone, a wimp with no goal in life and no idea what to do with himself. Presumably, he is supposed to grow into a man of character who has a profound relationship with people and is ever more deeply identified with God's will. This really never happens. Even on Palm

Sunday, when he stirs up the crowd to the fever pitch of rebellion, he suddenly wilts, wonders to himself what he is doing in front of the zealous eyes of the mob he has created—and walks away.

The film fails because it is gratuitously scandalous and blasphemous. It also fails because it takes a culturally corrupt approach to Christ's humanity. By choosing to present Jesus as a model of humanity at its worst, a person incapable of even the simplest acts of purpose and destiny, it fails at the outset to create any dramatic tension. Why tempt someone who is only too eager to give in? It's the *struggle* between good and evil that makes the moral life credible. Temptation is meaningless for a person who has never learned to love anyone but self, who has raised the white flag before the war ever started. Such a person is already a moral catastrophe. Character is destiny and the Jesus of this story has no character.

The Last Temptation

At first sight it seems that the four challengers in the Gospels set the agenda for the final temptation of Jesus. They frame the questions. They take themes from Christ's ministry—Messiah, king, divine Son—and use those images to force Jesus into saving himself instead of the world. They adopt a strategy that feels as new as today's self-absorption and as old as the biblical teaching about sinful selfishness. They might just as well have said, "Look out for number one."

Oddly, though, Jesus does not appear to be impressed with what they consider a devastating temptation. The evidence for the real temptation he faced is found in his first word: "Father, forgive them, they know not what they do" (Luke 23:34b). Apparently Jesus does not experience the temptation to save himself. (He faced and worked through that test at Gethsemane.) If he is experiencing any temptation at all, it is the urge to give up trying to save others. The temptation he feels is the temptation to refuse forgiveness.

The last temptation of Christ is the urge to forget about saving people or forgiving them. The duplicity, blindness, brutality and betrayal of those around him stimulate a vengeful reaction in him. He is human—like us in all things except sin. This means that he can experience the impact of temptations. He does so, however, as a fully integrated person in whom emotion and passion serve the purpose of loving others, bringing them peace and a sense of wholeness and rescuing them from all oppression, above all from the slavery of sin. Still, his integrated personhood does not absolve him from the impact of temptations.

Paradoxically, if he feels the urge to avenge he will know its seductive influence more acutely than anyone else. He is more aware of what it feels like to be vengeful than people who are practiced in nourishing and indulging their capacities for retribution. Integrity does not protect him from feeling; it opens him to it. The critical difference is that his integrity—ultimately based on absolute obedience to his Father's will—affords him the moral and spiritual strength to beat back the assault of temptations to destructive behavior. Jesus never sins. The brilliant Latin poetry of the Easter Sequence discloses his interior struggle for us:

> *Mors et vita duello*
> *Conflixere mirando.*

Death and life were locked together in a unique struggle.

Great saints give us a small hint of what this struggle must have been like in Jesus. It is more than a matter of living a disciplined life; the pagan Stoics could do that. It is a question of inner integration caused by divine love. The greater the union with Love, the more the saints are sensitive to the full import of temptations that come their way. The closer they are to God, the more intensely they feel the reality of sin and temptations to it. The vision of Isaiah (6:1-9) reveals the same phenomenon. The prophet, seeing the very holiness of God, intensely experiences the reality of sinfulness, so different from the purity of God. For shadows soften the outlines of things. Sunshine puts in bold relief both the good and the bad.

Provocations to Revenge

The whole passion story is full of provocations to revenge, to righteous anger and to retributive behavior.

Herod treats Jesus like a house clown. He wants Jesus to amuse him. "Herod was very glad to see Jesus; he had been waiting to see him for a long time, for he had heard about him and had been hoping to see him perform some sign" (Luke 23:8). Herod attempts to castrate Jesus psychologically by treating him in a humiliating way. "...Herod and his soldiers treated him contemptuously and mocked him" (Luke 23:11a). Herod tries to strip away Christ's human dignity more deftly than violent beatings by the soldiers promised to accomplish.

Christ's dramatic response is silence. The provocative situation called upon him to have feelings of anger, revulsion, revenge. Does Herod deserve forgiveness? Does he merit the offer of salvation? The silence of Jesus conceals the inner drama of his passion. Only when his first word issues from the cross do we know his response. Jesus had once preached, "...[L]ove your enemies, and pray for those who persecute you" (Matthew 5:44a). Jesus now witnesses to his own teaching. He preaches and he practices. His first word is not only a *teaching*, it is an *act* of forgiveness. Attractive as forgetting about forgiveness may have seemed, Jesus would have none of it. The only possible healing answer is a forgiving one.

The challengers at the cross all provoke him to a hostile response. Whom shall he forgive: the soldiers who punched him in the face? The religious rulers who ridicule his messiahship? The crowd who jeers at his divine sonship? The robber who curses him?

They have all battered his self-esteem. They have questioned the usefulness of his life, his career. The soldiers have beaten his body and tried to rob him of all self-respect. The leaders of religion have emptied his teachings of all relevance and meaning. They have persuaded people to disregard his message, to forget all about him, to mistrust him. The crowd has turned his miracles, meant to announce a kingdom of love, justice and mercy, into a sideshow for their amusement. From a potential community of faith and discipleship, they have turned into a mere mob. The criminal treats him as a denizen of a lower order than himself.

Shall he forgive people such as these?

Yes.

Why?

For they know not what they do.

If they were aware of what they were doing and persisted in it, they would be guilty of malice. If they understood they were abusing an innocent person and continued such behavior, they would be consciously immoral. If they appreciated that they were actually mocking and beating the real Messiah-king, the true Son of God, and pursued their destructive deeds, they would be responsible for their own actions.

Jesus forgave them because of their ignorance. The Church Fathers taught that the wound of ignorance results from original sin. That wound of ignorance brought Jesus to the cross and elicited from him an act of healing forgiveness. His death would strike at the cause of the wound: the fundamental sin that alienated people from Love.

One by one, Christ's disciples would repeat the understanding forgiveness expressed in his first word. Peter: "I know...you acted out of ignorance..."(Acts 3:17a). Stephen: "Lord, do not hold this sin against them"(Acts 7:60b). Paul: "At my first defense no one appeared on my behalf, but everyone deserted me. May it not be held against them!" (2 Timothy 4:16).

Forgiveness and the Healing of Persons

What else is salvation all about if it is not about the healing of persons? The soothing oil of forgiveness is at the heart of the saving act. Nothing regenerates a person better than being forgiven. Nothing more becomes the dignity of a person than the capacity to forgive. Virtually all wars and family splits and breakups of friendships can be traced back to the failure to forgive.

We all face one of the severest temptations in life, the seductive invitation not to forgive. We can think of a thousand reasons to avoid it. We believe forgiveness won't work. We have been betrayed too often. We will not trust in the power of loving forgiveness to solve a relational problem. We fail to believe in the inherent attractiveness of forgiveness and its intrinsic ability to heal.

In the days of our youthful idealism we asked ourselves, "What will convert the world?" Then we were willing to believe that love worked and that divine truth was inherently convincing. We grew older but not altogether wiser. Disappointments and betrayals took their toll. We allowed the cynics to write our agendas and gave up the dreams of youth—and lost our capacity to forgive and to accept forgiveness.

That is why Jesus held up a child for our admiration. He told us never to lose the youthful idealism that made it easy for us to believe in love's capacities. We should never let the child within us disappear. The last temptation we face is also the urge to refuse forgiveness.

For Reflection

1) The last temptation of Christ was the urge to refuse forgiveness of his persecutors. Jesus overcame that seduction and forgave his enemies. What people in your life can't you forgive? What excuses do you use to withhold forgiveness? Do you insist on an apology,

demand restitution, yearn for revenge?

2) If you expect forgiveness of your faults, failures and sins, do you think you can obtain this from Jesus while refusing to forgive others?

3) How do you feel when you have the willpower and the grace to forgive someone who has injured you?

4) What forgiveness stories in your experience strengthen your resolve to be a forgiver?

Prayer

Jesus,

I am grateful for your teaching about forgiveness
and your witness to that lesson.
I am tempted
as you were
to refuse to forgive those who have hurt me.
Bolstered by your influence on my life
I resolve to be a forgiver
even when it appears the other may not accept my offer.
I rest in your grace
and place all who have injured me
as well as those whom I have injured
in your hands.
Fill me with the Holy Spirit of reconciliation.

Amen.

People Only Listen to Witnesses

Amen, I say to you, today you will be with me in Paradise.

LUKE 23:43

The authorities crucified Jesus between two thieves. Placing him between two convicted criminals reinforced the impression of Jesus as a guilty man, not an innocent one. People had frequently criticized Jesus for seeking the company of sinners. Jesus had once replied, "I did not come to call the righteous but sinners" (Matthew 9:13). He now spends the final hours of his life between two of the lost sheep he had come to redeem. In his very act of saving all people he has the opportunity to save two of them in a uniquely personal way.

As we saw in the previous chapter, Christ spoke his first word of forgiveness in response to four challengers. They tempted him to save himself, thus provoking in him the temptation not to save them. He overcame that temptation and reaffirmed his commitment to redeem them. Now he is challenged to take his global offer of forgiveness and make it real and concrete in the interpersonal situation at Calvary.

One robber picks up the sarcastic chant of the religious rulers: "Are you not the Messiah? Save yourself and us" (Luke 24:39).

One might expect three condemned men facing imminent death to become a support group, each helping the other in a trying hour. Stripped of all other possibilities, they at least have each other and can form a community of the condemned. The living who stand around the crosses have a tomorrow to look forward to. Death awaits these three solitary figures. Why then would this thief lash out at one caught with him in the brotherhood of death?

No answer will ever prove satisfactory because the mystery of an individual conscience remains inaccessible to us—even more here because we have just one sentence from the thief's lips to go on. He has not told us his story. We know nothing of his family, his career, the demons that haunt him or the ideals that may have once inspired him. All we know is that he is a convicted thief and has delivered one angry, sarcastic remark to Jesus.

We may, however, be able in a general way to account for the anger in his tone by looking at the process of dying. Psychiatrist Elisabeth Kubler-Ross, who spent many years offering therapeutic consolation and support to dying people, has mapped out five turning points in the journey to death. Her descriptions ring true, even though there are exceptions and variations in the sequence. Her "stages of dying" are lamps of recognition that illumine our appreciation of the process of dying:

1) Denial: "No, not me. It can't be true."

2) Anger: experiencing the approach of death as a personal insult, an injustice directed toward us.

3) Bargaining: trying to stave off the inevitable, engaging in "unfinished business," putting our affairs in order and finding all kinds of last-minute things to do.

4) Depression: weariness, sadness.

5) Acceptance: letting go, letting be and letting oneself grow into the new life with God. People in acceptance seem already to have made the transition and are waiting prayerfully and peacefully for ratification.

In the light of this process, we can suggest that the angry

thief has just come to grips with the stark reality of death in front of him. He can no longer deny what will happen to him. That he should strike out with impotent rage at someone who loves him is not surprising. However unfortunate, that is a common and understandable reaction. The man knows not what he does. Christ's love and forgiveness remain available to him.

An Evangelist at Skull Hill

The angry thief needs conversion. He needs someone who will reach out to him and invite him to accept forgiveness and salvation. That intervention comes from a surprising and unexpected source—the other thief, whom tradition has named Dismas:

> "Have you no fear of God, for you are subject to the same condemnation? And indeed, we have been condemned justly, for the sentence we received corresponds to our crimes, but this man has done nothing criminal." (Luke 24:40-41)

This is the voice of a person who has arrived at the stage of acceptance. He is beyond denial, anger, bargaining and depression. He sees the present situation clearly. He has transcended his uncontrollable rage at imminent death and has the moral insight to admit that the court has justly condemned him for his crime. It is one thing to be judged by the civil authority, however. Now he knows he faces the judgment of God and consequences that are more enduring than the present pain and humiliation.

At Skull Hill itself Dismas acts like a Christian evangelist. He struggles for the soul of his fellow criminal. He is doing a lot more than stopping him from a mean-spirited assault on the obviously innocent Jesus. (They both knew that Pilate had washed his hands of this innocent man's blood.) Dismas appeals to his companion at two levels. First, Dismas confronts the other's moral conscience and reminds him to be honest about his behavior and its present outcome. Conversion usually includes a moral component and a challenge to ethical change.

More importantly, Dismas draws his companion to the deepest level of faith by asking him to acknowledge God, whose judgment is only moments away. His approach is a wonderful mix of tenderness and rough forthrightness.

The Gospel is silent about the reaction of the angry thief to the intervention of Dismas. He leaves us no testimony about how he felt and whether he accepted or rejected the invitation to faith. Many believe his silence means that he refused to repent. This has prompted some commentators to interpret the scene in terms of Christ's Last Judgment sermon (see Matthew 25:31-46). In this view Jesus is the judge and the two thieves respectively represent the sheep to be saved and the goats to be damned.

But no one knows, this side of heaven, what happened to the complaining thief. His silence has sealed the outcome of his life. Our best response is to match his silence with ours. We entrust him to God.

The likable robber wins our hearts with his practical friendliness for Jesus and his unambiguous attempt to convert his comrade to moral honesty and spiritual readiness for death. He captures our whole attention when he asks Jesus for salvation: "Jesus, remember me when you come into your kingdom" (Luke 24:42b).

As far as we can tell, Dismas has only known Jesus for a few hours. No record of any conversation between them exists. Jesus is not portrayed as having said anything to him or tried to evangelize him in any specific way. Possibly Dismas was detained in the same prison room as Jesus. Maybe Dismas saw the events at the Fortress Antonia that morning: the release of Barrabas, the presentation of Jesus crowned with thorns and robed in red to the mob, Pilate publicly washing his hands of the whole affair. Certainly Dismas had heard the forgiveness uttered from the cross.

One thing is sure. Dismas had enough time to see how

Jesus acted and how he responded to the indignities to which he was subjected. As far as we can tell, the only word Dismas heard from Jesus was the mercy statement. So, what is he left with? The behavior of Jesus, his wordless witness.

Paul VI has written that witness is an essential component for evangelization: "Modern people listen more willingly to witnesses than to teachers. If they do listen to teachers, it is because they are witnesses" (*On Evangelization*, 41).

Christian behavior is a silent, effective and powerful proclamation of the Good News. A Christian who radiates faith in a simple and unaffected way can exert a transforming influence on others. Perhaps that is what the United Nations had in mind when they invited Mother Teresa to address the General Assembly as part of its 40th anniversary celebration. She approached the podium where volumes of words had been spoken for four decades. She thanked her hosts for the honor and asked the members of the assembly to pick up a small card at their desks.

Then she said, "Let us pray." She proceeded to lead Christians, Moslems, Jews, Communists, Hindus, Buddhists and people of no known persuasion in the recital of the Prayer of St. Francis. With that she bade them God's blessings, said farewell and left. The whole experience was virtually a wordless witness accompanied by a few courtesies and the warmth of the Franciscan prayer. Her part in the ceremony lasted little more than five minutes. Her brief impact transcended hours of rhetorical strivings at that podium because the witness, like a laser beam, cuts through what words devoid of witness fail to achieve.

As Huston Smith puts it in *The Religions of Man*: "Whenever religion comes to life it displays a startling quality. It takes over. All else, while not silenced, becomes subdued and thrown without contest into a supporting role."

Dismas noticed the witness of Jesus and permitted that to transform him. He watched Jesus. What did Dismas see?

Journeying to Glory

How Jesus appeared remains an unknown to us. The Gospel writers refrain from literary or psychological descriptions of people. Christian art, drama, music, film and literature have attempted to fill in the gap. Icons and frescoes, Gothic sculptures and angular baroque paintings, Indian clay figures and African woodcarvings—from cathedral majesty to parish-church plain, a riotous pluralism represents the Christ of the Passion. And believers' creative impulses will continue. The Logos has become "flesh" in many ways since his first incarnation in Bethlehem.

Today photography provides another view. In 1960 Adam Bujak, a young Polish photographer from Kraków, decided to photograph the traditional rural rituals of Catholic Poland. Rather than arriving as an outsider taking pictures, he joined the people on their various pilgrimages and in their celebrations, many of which date from the Middle Ages. Only when he had earned their trust did they share with him their stories and experiences. Only then, when his presence was accepted, did he begin to take pictures. His "psychic" pictures remind one of the films of Ingmar Bergman.

With American journalist Marjorie Young, he published a book called *Journeys to Glory: A Celebration of the Human Spirit*. The third photo essay in it is titled, "The Celebration of the Sufferings of the Lord." It takes place in a small town deep in rural Poland. One hundred fifty thousand people have gathered there in Holy Week to reenact the Passion of Christ at the Chapel of the Council of the High Priests and Elders:

> They gather around a life-sized wooden statue of Jesus, whose hands are chained to a pole and on whose body wound marks can be seen. The statue portrays Jesus, not as an elegant figure, but as a simple peasant. Pilgrims place candles around him and talk to him as a friend. They stroke his face lovingly and tell him their

problems. Some ask for cures or to be able to see or hear better. Others kiss his hands and his face and prostrate themselves before him.

This is a world of genuine drama, emotion and meaning. It is a celebration of everyone's birth, death, triumphs and tragedies. Through the focus of Christ's Passion, universal experiences are lived anew. Celebrating them brings about a regeneration of the participants.

A 20th-century photographer and a journalist found themselves profoundly moved by a celebration of the sufferings of Jesus because they honestly opened themselves to the experience and gained the trust of the participants. One may suggest this is what happened to Dismas. Doubtless it was an act of grace as well. In the words of the old song, "Amazing Grace":

'Twas grace that taught my heart to fear,
And grace my fears relieved;
How precious did that grace appear
The hour I first believed!

Foundations of Conversion

Grace builds upon human experience in the process of conversion. Catholic University sociologist Dean Hoge has researched conversions to Catholicism and noted that certain conditions make the conversions more likely to happen.

The first condition is a *religious worldview*. This means the person believes in God and in general approves of values based on such a belief, even though such knowledge may be sketchy. In the present-day United States over 90 percent of Americans have this worldview.

In biblical times a religious worldview was virtually universal. Ideological atheism is an invention of the post-Enlightenment world. The good thief—and indeed, the other one as well—would have believed in a God and in a universe influenced by that divinity. God may not have influenced them very much, but they would have believed in God's existence nonetheless.

The second condition for conversion is a *felt need for a spiritual life* or involvement in a formal religion. This usually results from a "facilitating event" such as the birth of a child, marriage, the death of a loved one. At a less personal level, career changes, purchasing a home, "buying" into the local community, settling down at last are other experiences that could open one to conversion to a formal Church or to a deeper spiritual involvement.

The facilitating event in the life of Dismas was the raw fact he was about to die. Nothing so concentrates the mind as facing a gun pointed at one's heart. Death seems to cancel all other possibilities. It causes, as so many have testified, one's whole life to pass before one's eyes. It appears to have produced in Dismas the critical felt need for spiritual regeneration.

The third condition for conversion is meeting a *facilitating person*. One develops a bond of affection with a spiritual leader, a person of faith. Rarely does an institution or an ideology or a religious creed convert someone, mainly because the stimulus is too impersonal. Admittedly, intellectual conversions occasionally happen, but they are exceptions to the rule. The norm is that persons convert persons. The bonds of affection usually precede the bonds of membership in a Church.

Dismas had scarcely one day to develop a bond of affection with Jesus. Given the frenzied events that swept up Jesus and occupied his time, there were few opportunities for any kind of intimate relationship to develop between him and Dismas. Dismas had to be content with savoring the wordless witness of Jesus. We may conclude with confidence that Jesus became the facilitating person in the conversion of Dismas.

Silent Communion With a Hero

Dismas developed a silent bond of affection for one who is himself the source of all affection. This would not be the first case in history where there was silent communion with a hero figure.

Contemporary fashion, with its emphasis on the egalitarian model, tends to obscure this common experience. Heroes seem out of place in a culture where everyone ought to be the same size. Discovery of fatal flaws in many public role models reinforces our suspicion of the outsized hero.

Much of that cultural bias is to be commended, for in fact it provides a fresh look at the Jesus of the Passion. His heroism is not stoic resistance, not clenched-tooth defiance of pain. He reflects a deeper power: He concentrates on the spiritual uses of pain in the cause of restoring the primacy of love. He does not project the image of a colossus crumbling under the pressures of tragic forces.

What always continues to captivate believer and unbeliever alike is this image of a person apparently swept along by a sudden rush of inevitable events, yet slowing them down so as to incorporate them into a plan that will change the world. Culture associates heroism with feats of physical strength, dramatic confrontations with tyranny and courageous deeds of fearlessness in time or battle or in the saving of a person's life. And those are correct associations. Yet Jesus chose yet another form of heroism, not meant to eclipse those types, but to introduce a vision of the heroic which to the casual eye seems out of place in the pantheon of heroes.

St. Paul verbalized Christ's vision of heroism accurately in his letter to Corinth:

> ...God chose the foolish of the world to shame the wise, and God chose the weak of the world to shame the strong, and God chose the lowly and despised of the world, those who count for nothing, to reduce to nothing those who are something.... The message of the

Cross is foolishness to those who are perishing, but to
us who are being saved it is the power of God.

(1 Corinthians 1:27-28, 18)

Immediately, it must be said that Paul is not praising
foolishness, weakness and obscurity for their own sake. He is
claiming that salvation does not come from human
brilliance, however commendable, or from human health
and strength, however desirable, or from fame and its
positive uses, however admirable. A smart, strong and
famous preacher knows the powers at his disposal, yet does
not see them as the key to the victory of love.

There are lots of brilliant people who have never known
the joy of loving. The world is full of powerful people, many
of whom have no capacity for affection. The culture idolizes
countless members of the rich and famous whose personal
lives are sad testimony to a loveless existence. Paul says to all
of them that the message of the cross is foolishness to the
brilliant, weakness to the powerful and nothingness to the
famous. But to those who have discovered love, the cross is
the very power of God. Paul is not saying the bright,
powerful and famous cannot know love. He is reminding
them that the very keys to their worldly success may close
the doors on the fulfillment of their spiritual hungers.

Jesus is the Logos, the very essence of brilliance, yet he
seems to do something very foolish in allowing people in a
provincial backwater to kill him. Jesus is the Son of God, so
powerful that the very cosmos came into existence through
him, yet he looks weak when he lets the muscled soldiers
beat him. Jesus is the most famous man in Jerusalem on Palm
Sunday, acclaimed correctly as the Messiah-Savior, yet he
looks like a nobody on Good Friday when he permits the rich
and famous to crucify him.

Is this heroism? Yes. Love surpasses the capacity of
human wisdom to make a person feel whole again. Love
outperforms the ability of physical strength and political and
financial power to make a person feel truly secure. Love is far
more successful than fame in establishing a strong identity in

a person. The correct translation of the cross is love. That is why it has appealed from Good Friday to the present to the so-called foolish, weak and obscure of the world. These people surge around the cross to be loved and they feel, rightly, that they will not be disappointed.

Most of the wise, strong and famous people of the world have long since disappeared, save the few who make the history books—and their lives are often chronicled for being cautionary tales about the results of loveless witness. Jesus remains, not just as an inspiring historical figure, but as the inescapable presence of Love.

Dismas was a lucky man to have been able to have silent communion with his hero, who did not disappoint him. With joy, Jesus turned to him and said: "Amen, I say to you, today you will be with me in Paradise" (Luke 23:43).

Love offers us the same promise.

For Reflection

1) Dismas experienced a religious conversion at the cross. The conditions were just right: his religious worldview, his forthcoming death as a facilitating event, his experience of Jesus as a facilitating person. Have you been fortunate enough to experience a continuing moral and religious conversion throughout your life? What events have been occasions of conversion? What persons have influenced you to a deeper conversion to Christ and a more profound resistance to sin?

2) It is often said that the silent witness of lived Christianity is one of the most powerful ways to convert others to Christ. Name some examples of this in your own experience.

3) What about your own spiritual and moral witness? Has it exerted a converting influence on others, as far as you can tell?

Prayer

Jesus,

your words at the cross were more than sayings.
I see them as the actions of one
who witnesses what he teaches.
I am grateful to you
and to the people I have known
who have the moral and spiritual courage
to witness to teachings about love and salvation.
I ask you for this valued gift of spiritual witness.
I pray that my own witness
may have a saving influence on others.
Call me constantly to strong Christian witness.

Amen.

Unfinished Business

When Jesus saw his mother and the disciple there whom he loved, he said to his mother, "Woman, behold, your son." Then he said to the disciple, "Behold, your mother." JOHN 19:26-27a

The mother of Jesus stands below the cross with her sister, Salome, the wife of Zebedee and mother of James and John. Also there is Mary's sister-in-law Mary, the wife of Clopas (who was Joseph's brother) and mother of James and Joseph. There too are John, Zebedee's son and Jesus' cousin, and Mary Magdalene.

The setting for the third word is like the reading of a will. In an oral culture, the last testament is spoken; it is delivered before a person dies and in front of family witnesses. Jesus has some unfinished business to settle before he dies. Uppermost in his mind is the care of his mother. He does not let his present agony distract him from his duties as a son. Nor does he allow the cosmic nature of his crucifixion, the grand design to save the world, the global and historical reach of his redemptive purpose get in the way of his filial responsibility toward his mother.

He asks his cousin John to take care of his mother. From time to time the question arises as to whether Mary had other children besides Jesus. Catholic tradition firmly maintains that she did not. This scene appears to support the view that Jesus was her only child. If Mary had other children, would she not be entrusted to one of them by Jesus? "And from that hour the disciple took her into his home" (John 19:27b).

A Wedding and a Deathbed

Throughout his life, Jesus strove to illumine the divine meaning resting in the midst of visible events. In John's Gospel, after turning water to wine at Cana and feeding a multitude with five loaves in the wilderness, Jesus conducted a dialogue at Capernaum. He tried to lead his listeners to appreciate the gift of the Eucharist, symbolized by those two miracles. At Calvary, having ensured the security of his mother, he moves inside that event to bring out its more profound meaning. He turns to his mother and says, "Woman, behold, your son."

Hearing herself addressed as "Woman," Mary must have remembered Cana. Jesus had spoken to her with that title when she pointed out that the embarrassed couple was running out of wine.

Mary not only delighted in the wonder of her child as any mother would; she also enjoyed him in faith, watching the identity foretold by Gabriel unfold in his development: "He will be great and will be called Son of the Most High, and the Lord God will give him the throne of David his father, and he will rule over the house of Jacob forever, and of his kingdom there will be no end" (Luke 1:32-33).

Mary never forgot what the angel told her about him. Love gradually revealed to her, in a process that took years, the realization of those words in her son's life. She embarked on a faith journey from Nazareth to the Cross. She had been given a revelation about the mystery of her son, and she lived with it in faith and love. Living side by side with Jesus, under the same roof, year after year, persevering in union with her son, she made her pilgrimage of faith.

At Cana her faith moved her to ask Jesus to begin manifesting his saving presence and his public ministry of love. The heavenly Father had initiated him for his ministry at the Jordan baptism. The earthly mother interceded with him at Cana to start his active ministry. She wanted the messianic power of her son to be revealed. Jesus perfectly understood what she meant. Their communion as son and mother in an environment of faith assured that outcome.

His reply at Cana—that his hour had not yet come—indicated hesitation about deciding the proper time to start. The word *hour* here means more than clock time. It means right, suitable or proper time—what the Greeks called *kairos*, the fullness of time. Had Jesus concluded that Mary was only concerned with a pragmatic solution to the couple's problem (such as going out and buying some more wine), he would not have responded with messianic language about the "hour."

Moreover, it would then be unlikely that he would have used the title *woman* for her. Catholic commentators note that if he had called her "mother," he would be referring only to her physical parentage. By addressing her as "woman," he elevated her to a maternal role in the history of salvation. He spoke to her motherhood in the spirit, not just in the flesh, a motherhood that made her solicitous for people in the broad variety of their needs and wants, especially their fundamental need for salvation.

Mary invited her son to begin his saving work. He affirmed what her faith prompted her to do and celebrated her role as woman/mother/intercessor in the plan of salvation. Mary dispelled any hesitation about the "hour." She told the servers, "Do whatever he tells you" (John 2:5b). Jesus then performed the wine miracle. This was the first time he manifested his glory.

The biblical word for *glory* referred to the presence of God. The Old Testament used the word to refer to the radiant cloud that led Israel by day, the fire that walked before them by night and the shining cloud over the Ark of the Covenant. These visible signs awoke in the observers the feeling of God's presence, a presence that was loving and healing.

The glory invited them to deeper faith. That same experience occurred in the wine miracle, the first of the signs of Christ's glory—"and his disciples began to believe in him" (John 2:11b). Mary's faith preceded and interceded for the appearance of the glory. In a sense she was the first disciple who already believed in him. Her faith occasioned an event that evoked faith in others.

When Mary again heard her son call her "woman" at the cross, she recalled that formal beginning of the salvation process at Cana. She knew that the hour of salvation had reached its fullest realization at the cross. The two settings— Cana and Calvary, the wedding and the deathbed—are like an altarpiece, twin art works that belong together and have a unified message.

Mary's basic attitude from the Annunciation to the cross itself was always faith surrender: "Let it be done according to God's word." Her silence at Calvary gave consent. Rarely has the poetic symmetry of the divine plan of salvation been more tellingly visible in the Scriptures. The Catholic tradition of relating to Mary as our mother originates in this scene of the bequest, the third word.

Centuries of Christian reflection on this call to spiritual motherhood for Mary has resulted in relating her to other scriptural images of motherhood: Lady Zion, Eve and the woman clothed with the sun in Revelation. These symbols enrich our appreciation of the meaning of Mary's vocation as Mother of the Church.

Prayer Leader in the Upper Room

The second time we see Mary at intercessory prayer is in the Upper Room with the 120 disciples of Jesus during the nine-day "novena" before Pentecost. For these few days Mary is a public figure; her prayer witness is there for all to behold. She leads the way for the others, for she is more experienced in faith in Jesus than all of them put together. She is also more practiced in prayer. In a sense she is like a new Ark of the Covenant with the radiance of Christ's presence within her.

The 11 apostles were in that room. Jesus had promised them the Spirit who would send them out to evangelize the world. Their apostolic mission began when they left the Upper Room after the reception of the Spirit. Mary did not directly receive such a mission. She was not among those sent out into the world to teach all nations.

But she was in the Upper Room with the apostles and the other men and women when they prepared for their mission, devoting herself to prayer. The others knew she was the mother of Jesus, the author of salvation. They felt the special presence of a woman who was a unique witness to the mystery of Jesus from the moment of his conception.

Just as Mary was present at the conception and birth of Jesus, so she was present at the birth of the Church. The prayer group in the Upper Room gazed through Jesus at Mary and through Mary to Jesus. As the Church was coming to birth its members stood next to Mary, the first believer in Jesus, who already had a faith pilgrimage of 30-some years behind her. As they observed her they would be drawn to affirm what Elizabeth had said over three decades before, "Blessed are you who believed that what was spoken to you by the Lord would be fulfilled" (Luke 1:45).

Mary believed long before anyone else: at Nazareth, at Bethlehem, in Egypt, at the temple, at Cana, during Jesus' public ministry, at the cross where, like Abraham, she hoped against hope. Her faith did not fail at the cross. As Abraham became the father of faith for the people of the first covenant, Mary would become the mother of faith for the members of the Christian covenant. At Easter the promise of Nazareth rang like cathedral bells in her heart, for all she had believed came true.

At the birth of the Church on Pentecost, after her own lengthy faith pilgrimage, she joined those who would be the seed of the new Church, witnessing to them that a long pilgrimage of faith lay ahead. Mary had been present at all the key moments in the process of salvation from Nazareth to the Upper Room. There was an essential bond between Mary and the Church from the very beginning. That is why the Church never has forgotten her from generation to generation. "...[B]ehold, from now on will all ages call me blessed./The Mighty One has done great things for me..."(Luke 1:48b-49a).

The Outcome at Ephesus

Tradition maintains that John the Beloved brought Mary with him to Ephesus when he moved there. "The House of Mary" is now a pilgrimage site at Panya Kapulu in modern Turkey. It rests on a hillside overlooking the ancient city of Ephesus (present-day Seljuk). Her home is now a small fieldstone chapel visited by pilgrims—including Muslims, whose religion venerates Mary.

This tradition adds a special faith dimension to Christ's human request that John take care of his mother. In a few centuries Ephesus would be the site of a Council of the Church that forged a historic statement about Mary's relationship to her son and yielded her the title *Mother of God*.

Arriving with John at Ephesus, Mary would have seen the fourth largest city of the Roman empire—only Alexandria, Antioch and Rome itself were bigger. Soaring above the city was the Temple of Diana, one of the seven wonders of the world. Resting on a marble platform 400 feet long, the temple building covered an area larger than a football field. Its 100 columns rose to the height of a five-story building. Sculptures, paintings and gold plate adorned its walls. The Ephesians built their temple around a "sacred stone that fell from the sky," most likely a meteorite.

The temple housed a statue of the Ephesian Diana (they called her Artemis), the fertility goddess of Asia Minor. Mary could not have missed seeing the many gold and silver replicas of Diana displayed for sale throughout the city. They represented the goddess as a many-breasted figure, wearing a high crown decorated with the signs of the seasons. A purchaser would place the small statue in the Temple and provide an endowment to keep the image clean. On the goddess's birthday, the images were paraded through the city to the theater for a celebration.

The historical coincidence cannot be lost on us: Mary, the fruitful spiritual mother of Christians, moving to a home overlooking the city that worshiped a pagan fertility goddess.

Mary's sunset years, spent on a mountain overlooking the blue waters of the Aegean and the white-marbled city of Ephesus, left no record. We do not know what she was thinking. We know of no confidences she exchanged with John—or with anyone else, for that matter. Whatever faith-sharing took place just stayed right there.

Buried even more deeply is the silence of Mary's contemplative prayer and her heartfelt intercessions for the needs of the infant Christian community. At Cana and Pentecost it was evident Mary had acquired a habit of the heart that would endure forever, even after her glorious Assumption into heaven. Her prayers would be an essential complement to the scriptural writings of John and the evangelization ministry which would bring Paul to Ephesus. Mary's prayer would be the source of blessings for the living Church, surely part of the Spirit's gift to Paul when he wrote the majestic Letter to the Ephesians, celebrating that Christ's love makes possible the unity of all people regardless of their gender or ethnic origin.

During the life of the historical Jesus, Mary lived as Lady Zion amid her own people of the first covenant. After Easter and Pentecost, when the risen Christ had sent his Holy Spirit to be with the Church, Mary lived as the New Eve and the Apocalyptic Woman amid the Jews and Gentiles who professed faith in the Christian covenant. In a very special way, the Christian presence of Mary has endured as a special blessing at Ephesus from Easter dawn on through history.

Theotokos

If Mary had been given the gift of looking into the future—say, 400 years ahead—she would have seen a church that was a conference center for intellectuals in her lifetime. She would have heard they renamed this ecclesiastical setting the Mary Church; she would have noted a bustling assembly of bishops gathered to discuss her maternal relationship to her son.

In June 431 an ecumenical council was held there. Bishop Cyril came from Alexandria and Bishop John from Antioch. Pope Celestine sent two legates. Augustine planned to come, but he died before the council began. Over 200 bishops journeyed to Ephesus to celebrate their faith in Mary as Mother of God. Traditional Christian prayers addressed Mary with this title, but Nestorius, the patriarch of Constantinople, had posed a challenge to its usage.

At Ephesus the council fathers met this challenge. At stake was the central Christian truth that the man Jesus, son of Mary, is also truly the son of God. The Council reaffirmed that Mary may rightly be called the "Mother of God," not in the sense of having existed before God, but as an affirmation of the truth of the Incarnation. The son of Mary is one person, the Son of God, Emmanuel. Cyril of Alexandria spoke for the faith of the Church when he wrote:

> If we are to confess that Emmanuel is truly God, we must also confess that the Holy Virgin is *Theotokos* (Mother of God), for she bore according to the flesh the Word of God made flesh. Nor was he born of the holy Virgin as an ordinary man, in such a way that the Word only afterwards descended upon him. Rather he was united with flesh in the womb itself, and thus is said to have undergone birth according to the flesh, inasmuch as he makes his own the birth of his own flesh. For this reason the Fathers have boldly proclaimed the holy Virgin *Theotokos*.

Pope John XXIII chose the feast of Mary, Mother of God, as the day to open the Second Vatican Council. (At that time the feast was October 11. Today it is January 1.) On the vigil of the feast, 300,000 people crowded the square of St. Peter's. They carried lighted candles to brighten the evening, recalling a similar joyful celebration of *Theotokos* 15 centuries before.

They came to pray with Mary for blessings on the Second Vatican Council. Once again Mary, Mother of God and Mother of the Church, was invoked at a turning point in

Christian history. The smiling Pope John, standing on the balcony of St. Peter's and gazing out over the faithful community echoed the Third Word, "Woman, behold your sons and daughters."

The spirit of Ephesus spanned the centuries and rested upon the gathering who came to "open the Council," as Pope John said that evening. Grace and history transformed St. Peter's Square into a new Upper Room. The successors of St. Peter and the apostles were there. Three hundred thousand disciples were there. And Mary was there, leading them, as always, in prayer.

Teacher of Love

Jesus gave us Mary to be our mother. We have seen that she is a witness to faith and prayer for us. She also is a teacher of love—not because she speaks a lot of words about loving, but because she made in her life an interior space where love could grow and flow over into action.

Mary *decided* to love. We have been told often enough that love is a decision, not an emotion. If love depended on feeling, then we would not do much loving, because feelings come and go and negative feelings would drive us away from a person in need. Real love does not bother with reasons for loving others, but puts a lot of effort into finding ways to love people. The best love is a decision rooted in faith in God.

Mary faced the mystery of bearing a child without having had a husband. Simply and honestly, she asked the angel how this could happen. She was not closed-minded or upset about the mystery. Humanly speaking, she just wanted to know. God gave her a supernatural answer: The Holy Spirit would make it happen. That was enough for her. She made a love decision and accepted God's word. She bore a child not as the result of a human love act, but a divine love deed.

Just as faith grounded her love decisions so does it invite us to loving decisiveness. It has been said that rewards do not go to the timid. Neither are they distributed to the indecisive. Religious faith is the hidden heart of love decisions because it gives us the courage to become what God has planted within us from our conception and birth.

Mary practiced "letting-go" love. Human development expert Erik Erikson says that growth involves a crisis in which there are both identity loss and identity gain. Each time we gain in love there is some kind of loss. At Cana Mary had to do what every mother must face: let her son go off into his chosen career. Mary not only let Jesus go, she encouraged him to do so. She knew and faced directly the letting go that real love requires. She called him to embark on his messianic mission. He rewarded her by revealing to her a new way of loving. She would have more people to love than just her son. She would be spiritual mother of Jesus' brothers and sisters.

The cross challenged her to let go in a way she could never have anticipated. No mother wants to let her son die. No mother is anxious to release her child to death. When the knife of the Roman soldier pierced the side of Jesus, Mary felt it plunging into her own as well. When Jesus committed her to John's care, she heard him saying, "It is time for you to release me, to let me go into death."

Whatever interior struggle she experienced then remains private. The communion between herself and Jesus rests in impenetrable silence. We may correctly conclude, however, that she surrendered him then; she let him go. Love can do no other. Jesus then replied with the word that confirmed the love challenge he intimated at Cana when he called her "woman" for the first time. She will now be mother of the Redeemer—and of the redeemed.

John was faithful to Jesus' Third Word by accepting the responsibility to care for Mary. In turn, Mary fulfilled her son's request to become a spiritual mother to all believers. As Mother of the Church she witnesses faith for us and prays that our faith in Jesus will mature throughout every stage of our life journey.

For Reflection

1) When Jesus commended John to Mary, he was asking his mother to accept a special spiritual role toward every person who would be a disciple, to become the Mother of the Church. Though she is not mentioned often in the Scriptures, the times she is portrayed are central to salvation: Bethlehem, Cana, Calvary, Pentecost. What is your relationship to Mary? Do you ask her to pray for you, to help you get closer to Jesus? Does she inspire you to deeper faith and discipleship? Have you grown in appreciation of her faith relationship to her son?

2) No other human being in history spent more years, days and hours in personal proximity to Jesus than Mary. What can you do in your situation to draw closer to Jesus? Why would that be important to you? Why would that be important for your relationships with others?

Prayer

Jesus,

thank you for entrusting me
to the spiritual maternity of your mother, Mary.
Through faith I stand at the cross
and hear you ask Mary to look out for me.
I read the Scriptures
and see what kind of a woman she was—
a person of deep faith and a habit of prayer.
I ask Mary to pray for the deepening of my faith
and for the gift of prayer.
Then I can become your disciple
in the best sense of the word.

Amen.

'I Want to Feel Your Presence'

My God, my God, why have you forsaken me? MATTHEW 27:46b

Four soldiers guarded the cross. Jesus watched them discuss how they would divide his clothes among themselves. As a typical Jewish man, he would have had five pieces of apparel: a turban or hood for his head, sandals for his feet, a tunic to cover his body, a belt to cinch the tunic and an outer cloak or robe. His cloak was a seamless robe, probably woven by his mother. The four soldiers settled on the allocation of four of Christ's garments and threw dice for his robe.

Jesus went to his death as a priest: High priests wore seamless robes. Josephus described the ankle-length tunic of the high priest as one long woven cloth, not composed of two pieces. The priest Aaron, Moses' companion, wore such a woven robe: "For Aaron and his two sons there were also woven tunics of fine linen..." (Exodus 39:27).

The Book of Revelation portrays Jesus as wearing the garments of both a king and a priest: "[I saw]...one like a son of man, wearing an ankle-length robe, with a gold sash around his chest" (Revelation 1:13b). The royal sash signified his kingship and the robe his priesthood. The high priest wore this "robe of reconciliation" when he stood before God celebrating a ritual meant to create harmony between God and the people. Jesus also wore the robe of harmony as the high priest who would establish the possibility of universal reconciliation.

Now Jesus gazed at the soldiers insensitively gambling for his clothes right in front of him as his life ebbed away. The scene must have reminded him of a verse from Psalm 22, which is the prayer of an unknown martyr and a prayer often used by those faced with personal pain and death. The martyr spoke of his life ebbing away like water and of the racking of his bones. He felt his heart melting as though it were wax. He complained that his throat felt like baked clay and his tongue stuck to the sides of his jaws. Jesus felt exactly the same way. The words of the old martyr expressed his own experience even more vividly as he watched the soldiers gambling for his priestly robe:

> They look on and gloat over me;
> They divide my garments among them,
> and for my vesture they cast lots. (Psalm 22:18b-19)

The absolute imminence of his death, coupled with the accumulation of indignities, plunged him into the depression so many face in the dying process. Even with his mother and dearest friends beside him, he felt the sense of isolation and loneliness that closes in on a dying person. Above all he felt the loss of God's presence. Like so many before him who had turned to Psalm 22 to express their deathbed sense of abandonment, Jesus cried out in a loud voice, " *'Eli, Eli, lema sabachthani?'* which means, 'My God, my God, why have you forsaken me?' " (Matthew 27:46b).

Commentators agree that Jesus most probably recited the entire psalm, which ends with an expression of trust:

> You who fear the LORD, praise him;
> ...For he has not spurned nor disdained
> the wretched man in his misery....
> The lowly shall eat their fill;
> they who seek the LORD shall praise him:
> "May your hearts be ever merry!"
>   (Psalm 22:24a, 25a, 27)

The psalm enabled Jesus frankly to share with his listeners

his experience of painful abandonment as well as his firm conviction that God will ultimately deliver him.

It is not surprising that Jesus would quote a Scripture passage at length. Jesus knew the Scriptures and let the word of God echo in the well of his soul. Listeners often heard the word from his lips, along with an original interpretation (see, for example, the Sermon on the Mount, Matthew 5—7).

Jesus knew this was the fulfilling hour. He embodied the scriptural words with the originality of his behavior, giving them their ultimate meaning. His obedience to his Father's will began in his heart and stood behind the words on his lips and the behavior all could see in his ministry, even to this moment. The silences of his passion expressed the same obedience. "I was speechless and opened not my mouth,/ because it was your doing" (Psalm 39:10).

Christ's attention to what was happening was probably never so sharp, so concentrated. The Jesus who recited Psalm 22 was a person totally present to himself, completely aware of what he was experiencing. Living the scriptural words was now a visible, audible and total act of integration for all to note. The clarity of the cry and the memory its impact caused in the listeners affirms his heightened consciousness. The speaking, the doing and the full commitment of his heart constituted the seamless robe of his personhood.

In meditating on the cry of abandonment, we should never forget that the conclusion of Psalm 22 praises the God who does not turn away from the martyr. We will return to that section in a moment. Meanwhile, two other comments must be made.

First, Jesus has not lapsed into temporary atheism. The ending of the psalm makes it clear that Jesus is not identifying with atheistic despair. Jesus is experiencing an assault of something more like spiritual aridity.

On the other hand, Jesus is not dispassionately reciting a conventional prayer of the dying. His use of the words is far more than an act of piety, however commendable. The text that lies so quietly on the page is more akin to a brutal shout than a reverent whisper. Jesus startled his audience with a passionate outcry that lets them know his dying is a serious business; his feeling of divine abandonment is starkly real. His pain breaks through the majestic silences of the Passion. He describes his loss of the sense of God's loving and protective presence.

The Death of God

In the 19th century, Frederick Nietzsche described the loss of a sense of God's presence in a parable about a madman:

> Have you not heard of the madman who lit a lantern in the bright morning hours? He ran to the marketplace and cried incessantly, "I seek God! I seek God! Where is God? I shall tell you. We have killed him, you and I. All of us are his murderers. The holiest and most powerful has bled to death under our knives. Who will wipe the blood off us?"
> Here the madman fell silent and looked again at his listeners. They, too, were silent and stared in astonishment at him. At last he threw down his lantern on the ground and it broke and went out. "I came too early. My time has not yet come." On that same day the madman entered various churches and there sang his *requiem aeternam deo (Eternal rest be unto God)*.

Critics of the sins of institutional religion and the hypocrisies of ostensible Christians used Nietzsche's image of the death of God to describe the disappearance of the sense of the divine presence which such behavior caused. They attributed the loss of the feeling of the holy to Christian leaders and believers who no longer witnessed love, justice, peace and salvation from all oppression, especially sin. According to them, the presence of God had departed from the churches.

That criticism, first launched in the 19th century, appeared again in the middle of the 20th. It acquired popular prominence when *Time* featured the idea on its 1966 Easter cover. Red text on a field of mourner's black asked, "Is God Dead?" The editors said that the question tantalizes both believers, who perhaps secretly fear that God is dead, and atheists, who possibly suspect that the answer is no.

The editors missed the point because they looked at the phenomenon in terms of God's *existence* instead of God's *presence*. The difference between existence and presence provides a context for Jesus' cry from the cross.

In the United States, virtually all people believe in God's existence. Studies show that half of them, however, testify to little or no experience of God's presence. The other half— mostly churchgoers—feel God's nearness in varying levels of intensity. Most Americans believe in God. They do not need proofs for God's existence. Similarly, almost everyone believes in love. Yet too many claim they have never been loved or do not know how to love themselves or anyone else.

Love demands presence. The whole point of the "God is dead" movement was that a great number of people were hungering for a personal God and instead were being given the abstract God of philosophy. People were searching for the God of the Bible, a covenant God who would be loving and present and touchable and feelable.

Ten years later, many young people were becoming "Jesus freaks" and their parents were joining religious enthusiasm movements such as the charismatic renewal, Marriage Encounter and Cursillo. In these movements no one talked about the aridity of needing God near their hearts. Now they celebrated in joyful songs, hymns, hugs and handclasps the surprising and unexpectedly powerful presence of the Holy Spirit. Evangelical fervor replaced abstract dryness, though it ran the danger of going to another extreme: emotionalism without intellectual reflection.

Nonetheless, personal experience of God renewed the faith that was in danger of dying. The crisis of God's presence subsided as the enthusiasm movements flourished and churches learned how to celebrate a personal God who calls people to love one another and bring justice to the world.

Jesus experienced God's abandonment of him in two ways. Objectively, God does not intervene to save Jesus' life. God lets Jesus go through with his death.

Subjectively, Jesus experienced the absence of the Father. As Son, he felt a sense of filial loss just when he most wanted his Father's assuring presence. Jesus basically said, "I want to feel your presence." In asking his Father why he withdrew his presence just when it would be most appreciated, Jesus joined ranks with all human beings who search for reasons for the trials that beset them. Jesus thus let us know how very much he is one of us when it comes to unraveling the mystery of human suffering. Even he hit a stone wall when challenged to penetrate the significance of personal tragedy.

Like all the rest of us, Jesus also found himself crying out, "Why, God?" Just as his human resistance to death at Gethsemane prompted him to ask that the cup not be given to him, so the lonely psychological encounter with the mystery of suffering on the cross motivated him to shout his *why*. Yet at Gethsemane he obediently surrendered to his Father's will. On the cross, he trusted that the Father would deliver him, if not from suffering and dying then in some after-death liberation. Obedience and trustful surrender to his Father's will was his fundamental attitude to the mystery of his suffering, death and abandonment.

The Ultimate Emptying

In his letter to the Philippians, Paul inserted a hymn about Christ's journey from divine glory to the humiliation of the cross. One of the earliest sung confessions of faith, this text applies to the cry from the cross:

> Who, though he was in the form of God,
> did not regard equality with God something to be
>   grasped.
> Rather, he emptied himself,
> taking the form of a slave,

coming in human likeness;
and found human in appearance,
he humbled himself,
becoming obedient to death,
even death on a cross. (Philippians 2:6-8)

The hymn opens with an act of faith in Jesus' divinity. It proceeds to praise Christ for divesting himself of the privilege of divine glory in becoming a human being. Jesus did not empty himself of divinity, but of status: the glory to which he had a right and which would be restored to him at his exaltation.

Jesus became a real human being. He chose a life of humility and obedience—not ordinary obedience, but heroic submission to his Father's will that led to death on the cross. He journeyed as far as he could from his celestial rights and glory. The image of physical distance helps to understand what has happened to him, but such a spatial picture does not satisfy the reality of what he did. Who can explain the nature of the gulf one feels when love seems to disappear? Jesus emptied himself to the point where even the presence of God is denied him. That is the ultimate emptying.

The Wounded Healer

In recent years the fascination with the physical brutalities of the Passion has yielded to a meditative preoccupation with Christ's inner drama. Many find as much faith nourishment in contemplating the interior wounds of Jesus as others have in reflecting on his five physical wounds. Father Henri Nouwen drew our attention to this with a persuasive image: the "wounded healer." The expression gives a contemporary ring to the ancient aphorism of St. Athanasius, "The unassumed is the unhealed." Father Gerard O'Collins puts yet another spin on this teaching when he says that "The uncrucified is the unhealed." All three variations enrich in still another way

47

our contemplation of the cry from the cross.

Jesus became the wounded healer in three ways.

1) He permitted his defenses to crumble. Like any human being, he had protective mechanisms, walls to defend himself against intrusive people. In his life, he let those walls fall away.

2) As his defenses withered away, he opened himself to both others' affection and their mistreatment. People could love him effectively. They could also betray and murder him.

3) He cured the wounders. The natural reaction to being hurt is to fight back and get revenge. But once Jesus permitted others to hurt him he took responsibility for the wounder. He paid less attention to his own pain and set out to heal the hurter. Whoever tried to disable him found in him not an enemy but a healer.

Jesus had preached love and forgiveness for enemies. On the cross, the wounded one became the Savior. His yell of abandonment let sinners know how he felt about the effects of their sins, even though he had already forgiven them for not realizing what they were doing. The impact of their sinfulness made him feel lonely for God because the experience of their sinfulness deprived him, momentarily, of the loving presence of his Father.

The brutal sound from the cross made it clear he felt the wounds. The stirring conclusion of Psalm 22 issued another sound, the voice of healing forgiveness. Jesus knew the moment of horror, the path of the walking wounded. He did not let such desolation absorb him in self-pity. Darkness may have covered Skull Hill, but it did not blind Jesus the Savior.

As Jesus reflected on the final words of Psalm 22, he seemed to relax and open himself to the last wound that evil can inflict, death itself. He praised his Father, not for delivering him from present agony or for restoring his sense of God's consoling presence. Jesus praised God for the healing of the world's sin his death would accomplish.

Jesus now can identify with the last invocation of Psalm 22: "May your hearts be ever merry!" The bells of Easter seem already to ring in his heart. He has passed over the temptation to strike out at his wounders. He is now able to offer them the grace of healing. Nothing can stop the momentum of salvation. He will speak no more of his anxieties or cup of pain.

In healing those who wounded him, Jesus offered evil people the chance to be transformed into good ones. He took sinners to his heart so that he might make them into new people. He offered them the love that cures irrational evil and motiveless malignity. If the unassumed is unhealed, the assumed is redeemed. If the uncrucified is alienated, the crucified is saved. If the healer refuses to be wounded, how can the wounder be healed?

Shakespeare said that for romantic lovers, love is blind. But Jesus is not a romantic lover on the cross. Far from being blind, his love is visionary. It enables people to see. Paradoxically, he is never more truly the divine-human lover than at this time. Just when his divine glory seems most lost and obscured does it become as perfectly apparent—and in complete unity with his humanity—as it could be before his resurrection.

Because salvation is achieved by love, the sinner cannot be forced to accept it. Jesus does not compel acceptance. He is as vulnerable to our refusal as he is to our acceptance. He taught that the truth makes us free. He then proceeded to identify himself as the living truth. He would make us free, not by forcing us to believe in him but by inviting us to accept love and know freedom.

The Incarnation, barely glimpsed in the baby at Bethlehem, is as fully revealed as it ever would be during Jesus' earthly life just after the cry of abandonment. That is why God's peace seems so palpable as history's greatest act of reconciliation comes to its fulfillment. John's Gospel teaches that the lifting up of Jesus on the cross is also his lifting up to glory. Cana was the first of the signs whereby

Jesus manifested his glory, but the cross is the last and greatest sign.

'Pass the Cross to Me'

In the musical *Shenandoah* there is a song titled, "Pass the Cross to Me." The title seems to be a fitting conclusion to the meditation on Christ's fourth word. When Jesus offers us love and forgiveness, he also presents us with a spiritual and moral challenge. All of Luke's Gospel shows how one can become a disciple of Jesus. The song of the disciple, in Luke's view, would be, "Pass the Cross to Me."

Jesus invites us to be healed and then to be wounded healers. Just as he opened himself to receiving the love and affection of others, so should we. Just as he also made himself vulnerable to others' wounding him, so must we gradually be seasoned in accepting the wounds that come our way. This should not be some perverse form of self-punishment. Our purpose must be medicinal, intending to offer others Christ's salvation. Just as he transformed the hurters into the saved (when they were willing), so we also, by his love, will engage in that transforming Christian activity.

In the process we may have to let out our own yell of abandonment as we wonder what has happened to God's presence. Then it is we may find the inner strength to speak about a merry heart, for in our brokenness we will have found out how to heal others.

For Reflection

1) Jesus' cry of abandonment from the cross was not about the existence of God but about feeling the loss of God's presence. Do you sometimes lose the sense of God's presence? How do you react? When in your life have you felt God close? Do you expect the experience of God's presence always to be consoling?

2) Jesus was a wounded healer. He permitted others to get
close to him whether that be by affection or betrayal.
When they wounded him, he sought to heal them instead
of hurting them. Do you build a wall around yourself so
that no one can hurt you? Is your protective covering also
preventing people from touching you with love? How
could you become a wounded healer?

Prayer

Jesus,

your cry from the cross assures me
that even you know what it is like
not to feel God's presence.
Your confidence that God is there
even when the presence is momentarily gone
assures me that I shall be able to live
through times of suffering and puzzlement.
Further, your example of being a wounded healer
is a grace that I yearn for.
Bless me with trust in dark hours
and the capacity to heal when I am hurt.

Amen.

'Let Me Love You'

I thirst. JOHN 19:28b

Matthew and Mark report two different presentations of wine at the cross. When the procession arrived at Calvary, a guard offered Jesus wine mixed with myrrh, a flavoring that made the sour wine more palatable. Myrrh also was a narcotic meant to dull the prisoner's pain. Sometime later, a soldier presented him with a second drink of wine, this time on a stick of hyssop. Jesus tasted the first offering but did not drink it, possibly because he did not want a narcotic. He refused the second presentation of wine.

John's Gospel tells of only one presentation. Jesus asked for it and drank it. Throughout his ministry Jesus had used the image of drinking the cup to describe his commitment to the cross that was so essential to his saving ministry. Telling Peter to sheathe his sword at the arrest in Gethsemane, Jesus asked, "Shall I not drink the cup the Father gave me?" (John 18:11b). According to the other evangelists, at Gethsemane Jesus asked his Father if it were still possible to avoid drinking the cup:

> I only want to say
> If there is a way
> Take this cup away from me
> for I don't want to taste its poison.
> 			(*Jesus Christ Superstar*)

Nonetheless, in that garden prayer Jesus resolved to do his Father's will.

To Calvary the executioners brought a jug of soldier's wine—John calls it "common wine," a rough fluid with a vinegary taste that probably helped settle their own nerves during their grisly task. As Jesus drank that bitter wine, he demonstrated his determination to taste the death that would complete his saving mission.

The use of a sponge-tipped hyssop branch to present the wine introduced the healing symbolism associated with that plant. Biblical folk medicine prescribed the use of bird's blood soaked in hyssop to try to cure leprosy, albeit unsuccessfully. In Egypt the Israelites had dipped hyssop in lamb's blood and splashed it on their doors to avert the angel sent to slay all the firstborn children in the kingdom.

Psalm 51 remembers David's prayer that God would cleanse his soul from sin and guilt by flaying it with a hyssop branch, thus endowing the plant with moral significance. The medical, moral and salvational associations with hyssop in biblical memory cannot escape notice when that branch is used to present wine to Jesus, the lamb of God about to take away the sin of the world.

Scourged and Crowned

Heavy blood loss causes severe dehydration. The scourging at the pillar and the crowning with thorns is the reason for Jesus' physical thirst.

To scourge a victim, the Romans used a leather whip to which were attached a lead ball and a jagged piece of bone. The lead added to the impact to increase the bruising. The bone tore at the victim's flesh. They customarily bound the victim to a pillar nude, arms up. Though the law prescribed 39 lashes, more may have been administered to Jesus to ensure his death before sundown at Passover. The Roman executioners needed to hasten the death process in this crucifixion.

The Romans regularly scourged victims before crucifixion. The Gospels do not dwell on this scene or draw any religious message from it. But Christian piety, especially since the Middle Ages, has prayerfully contemplated this beating of Jesus. (Our more fastidious culture declines to linger on this bloody event, though it tolerates pervasive and meaningless bloody mayhem on the screen.) Christian believers have found a link between the torture of Christ's body and their own sins of the flesh. The power of the scourging, seen in this light, has motivated many believers to master the weaknesses of their fleshly passions and turn their desires toward the proper use of their bodies. Instinctively, they have understood the New Testament contrast between spirit and flesh, wherein spirit stands for strength and flesh is identified with weakness:

> The spirit is willing, but the flesh is weak.
> (Matthew 26:41)

> For if you live according to the flesh, you will die, but if by the spirit you put to death the deeds of the body, you will live. (Romans 8:13)

With St. Paul (see 1 Corinthians 9:27), these Christians engage in "temple maintenance," often honoring their bodies with healthful exercise and even more frequently with spiritual exercise so that their bodies may be true temples of the Holy Spirit. Admittedly, some believers have extended this legitimate application of the flesh-spirit teaching to a morbid hostility to both the body and sex. This aberration, however, should not justify ignoring a clear teaching of the New Testament or a sound tradition of Christian asceticism.

At the Last Supper, Jesus said that the cup is a covenant of the blood that he would shed for us. Christ's bloody Passion began at the pillar where the scourging literally drew his blood. A major cause of his physical thirst, the scourging also vividly illustrates what Jesus would undergo to make the everlasting covenant of love possible.

After the scourging, the soldiers devised a crowning with thorns as part of their traditional game of "Mock the King." Roman legionaries have left etchings pertaining to this game on the paving stones of the Fortress Antonia. Normally, the soldiers would place a papyrus crown on the "king's" head, a reed in his hand and a royal red cloak on his shoulders. They may have seen pantomimes like this at the circus or on the stage. The historian Philo records a mockery of Herod Agrippa I which was enacted on an Alexandrian stage. In it a lunatic named Karabas was decked out as King Agrippa and then saluted, consulted and acclaimed in a farcical manner.

At the Fortress Antonia, however, their mockery took a crueler turn most likely because Jesus was already beaten and bloody. The soldiers did not choose the playful papyrus but thorns. Long-thorned branches used for fires were readily available in the courtyard. Using a stick to fix the thorns, the crowner molded them into a cap over Jesus' whole head, which then bled profusely. That is how the crowning became the second major reason for the physical thirst of Jesus.

Some have speculated that the branches came from a date palm which has thorns near its base. If so, Good Friday presents a poetic symmetry with Palm Sunday. The branches of glory waved before Christ in his triumphal entry into Jerusalem became the branches of pain driven into his head.

The crowning mocked Christ's royal claim. Meant to symbolize the rays of light that flowed from the head of a divinity, the thorns formed the likeness of a king's crown. Seeking to be as rude as they knew how, the mocking soldiers knelt before Jesus and derisively hailed him as a king. Yet that same Gentile militia became the first people shaken into faith by the revelatory events of the cross:

> The centurion and the men with him who were keeping watch over Jesus feared greatly when they saw the earthquake and all that was happening. And they said, "Truly, this was the Son of God!" (Matthew 27:54)

Jesus is as anxious for us to love ourselves as we think we are, but he really wants real love, not a utilitarian approach to ourselves. It is he who made it possible for us to say, "I believe in the resurrection of the body." One step in making that possible was accepting the scourging of his body in order that our bodies may be healed of sinfulness.

God gave us a mind that was meant to be a creative echo of the Word of God. At the core of this precious gift of intelligence resides the drive to make truth and the values based upon it present in our lives. The Word of God was so creative that everything that exists flows from it. The Word performed this truth in love and out of love for us.

When we permit our minds to dwell on falsehood and to lapse into a conviction that truth is not possible, we betray our intelligence. We lose the possibility of doing the truth in love. We thus replace creativity with destructiveness. We lose the ability to consider how to love and acquire the habit of wondering how to use and exploit others. In its worst form this becomes ideology, so evident in the soul-destroying cultures that have tyrannized over half the people on earth for most of this century.

To heal this misuse of the mind the Word Made Flesh permitted the crown of thorns to be placed on his head after a discussion with Pilate about truth. This was a major step in healing human intelligence and restoring it to its proper function as a participant in doing the truth in love.

The Mysticism of the Passion

Many Christians have found meaning and strength in the mystery of the scourging and the crowning. As Jurgen Moltmann notes in *The Crucified God*, the poor, the sick and the crushed perceive the God of the poor as the suffering and unprotected Jesus. They believe that their wounds are healed by Christ's wounds. Pilate presented the scourged and crowned Jesus to a hostile audience and proclaimed, "Behold, the man" (John 19:5b). Unmoved, the mob called for his judicial murder. But faith-filled slaves and peasants from ancient times to our own day gaze on that helpless figure and begin to feel strong and renewed. A Lutheran martyr to the Nazis, Dietrich Bonhoeffer, has expressed their sentiments:

> God lets himself be pushed out of the world onto the cross. He is weak and powerless in the world, and that is precisely the way in which he is with us and helps us. Matthew 8:17 makes it clear that Christ helps us, not by virtue of his omnipotence, but by virtue of his weakness and suffering. Only the suffering God can help. That is a reversal of what the religious man expects from God. Man is summoned to share in God's sufferings at the hands of a godless world.
> (*Letters and Papers From Prison*)

The poor and suffering of this world tend to understand Jesus better than those who ignore or oppress them. Their situation moves them to identify with Jesus. Prosperous Christian cultures consider Easter and Christmas the highlights of the Church year. But in Latin America, Holy Week is the feast of the poor. They know how to share in the suffering and death, pain and mourning of Jesus. That Jesus is at home with them. The scourged Jesus brings healing to those who are beaten. The Jesus crowned with thorns brings God to those who suffer. The dying Jesus brings life to those who are dying. The rejected Christ, the wounded healer, stands with the lost and gives them hope.

The same faith shows in the black spirituals, slave songs from the American South. Filled with an immediacy that identifies the slaves directly with Jesus, the spirituals are a living dialogue: "Were you there when they crucified my Lord?" Yes, we were. "Were you there when we laid him in the tomb?" Yes, we were. They are at Christ's side; Jesus is at their side. History collapses when the Passion of Jesus and the passion of oppressed peoples coincide.

Other social critics agree with Marx that religion is the opium of the poor. They mean that religion has used the teaching of the cross to keep the poor submissive. "Carry your cross here. You will gain heaven in the hereafter. Don't try to obtain a better life for yourselves on earth."

At times that has been tragically true. But the Passion of Christ was never meant to justify injustice and oppression. Christ embraced the indignities of the Passion to liberate humans from all that oppresses them, whether that be social injustice or personal sin.

Those who preached that the cross demands craven submission to an unjust order should have been proclaiming the cross of detachment from greed to the rich; the cross of humility to the proud and powerful; the cross of justice, compassion and solidarity with the poor to the power-brokers.

Still, the perversion of the message of the cross on the part of some should not obscure the poor's authentic religious insight about the crucified Christ. They do not see in Jesus just another wretched person like themselves. They find in Jesus a God who does not oppress them, but becomes a loving brother and comrade. Circumstances have deprived them of freedom and human dignity. Jesus makes them feel free, humanly important and hopeful. They find a fresh and attractive identity in the Christ who suffers with them. They discover something Marx never understood: a sense of being loved by Jesus. Gazing upon Jesus scourged and crowned with thorns, they feel they need not sink back into misery.

This contemplation does not explain to them the meaning of evil or necessarily even provide them with a practical solution to life's problems. But such meditation establishes the possibility of doing so, for it affirms in faith that evil has been mysteriously overcome.

The cross introduces its own mystery. It does not erase the problem of evil. It liberates the poor from passive submission to fate and from apathy in suffering. Just as Jesus was actively involved in his own suffering, so the poor who appreciate the cross are actively involved in theirs. That leads them to seek freedom from injustice and to assert their human dignity.

The Spiritual Meaning of Christ's Thirst

Acute thirst is not easily ignored. Lawrence of Arabia wrote about its consuming power after a friend died of thirst in the desert:

> Thirst was an active malady, a fear and a panic that tore at the brain and reduced the bravest man to a stumbling, babbling maniac in an hour or two. Then the sun killed him.
>
> (*Seven Pillars of Wisdom*)

Maddening though his thirst may have been, Jesus did not yield to impulse in uttering his fifth word. John's Gospel presents a Jesus who presides over his dying process. The more intense the physical inhibitions, the more evidently his concentration dominates the experience of dying. As Jesus once explained to some Pharisees, no one will take his life from him (see John 10:18). He will surrender it when he is ready. He will control his death experience. When he spoke, therefore, he spoke with a spiritual purpose, as one in command of his last moments.

If any single theme dominated the ministry of Jesus, it was his desire for souls. This desire is the key to the meaning of his fifth word.

The unrestricted drive of Jesus' life was to give love to others and enable them to love God in return. Once, when his disciples offered a meal, he pushed aside the food and gazed in his imagination at a field of grain that needed harvesters. He told them that his real hunger was for harvesting souls for the kingdom of love. He said that even though God is both the sower and the reaper of the harvest of salvation, the Lord wants us to be the ministers that reach out and bring people to love (see John 4:31-38).

Just as the dividing of his garments reminded Jesus of Psalm 22, his physical thirst prompted him to recall the psalms of thirst, the songs of desire. Master of the covenant people's prayerbook, Jesus took possession of the words of

Psalm 69:22b, "[I]n my thirst they gave me vinegar to drink." As he contemplated the immortal words of that psalm he identified with them and endowed them with a meaning not envisioned by the psalmist.

His whole soul prayed the opening lines, which envision the destructive force of waters, the waters of chaos that threatened his life and offered no consolation to his parched throat. The destructive waters included those who insulted him and God, those who sat at the city gates and gossiped about him instead of believing in him, the drunkards who made him the butt of their jokes in taverns and missed his offer of saving friendship.

He was not immune to the curses of others, even if he forgave them. "Insult has broken my heart...," he prayed. "I looked for sympathy, but there was none..." (Psalm 69:21a,b). Jesus was not above wanting affection and love from others. He was no stern Stoic so absorbed in self-mastery that the kindness and embraces of others meant nothing to him. Determined as he was to bring love to others, he was equally thirsty for love from them. In his fourth word, Jesus yearned for the loving presence of God. In his fifth word, Jesus groaned for the loving presence of humans.

But just as Psalm 22, the cry of abandonment which was the fourth word, ends with a joyful affirmation of God's promised deliverance, so also Psalm 69 concludes with words of praise for the God who will hear the cry of the poor. It even repeats the sentiments of merriment found in Psalm 22: "[Y]ou who seek God, may your hearts be merry!" (69:33).

In the Gospel, "one of them ran to get a sponge. He soaked it in wine, and putting it on a reed, gave it to him to drink" (Matthew 27:48). Many commentators believe this unnamed responder to Christ's predicament was most likely one of the four soldiers guarding the cross. The guards maintained official control over contact with Jesus and they had, as we noted earlier, a jug of sour wine for their own use during the death watch. The Gospel records that the person went *running* to do this mercy, suggesting he was a younger member of the team of guards. Whoever he was, his action brought a trace of compassion to Skull Hill.

Christ had thirsted for evangelists to witness the gospel and for believers to accept him. He also thirsted for a little human affection. "I looked for sympathy..." (Psalm 69:21c). He found it in the tender response of that Roman soldier.

A Holy Impatience

The thirst of Jesus asked acceptance of his love from every human being: "Let me love you." Since the acceptance of love must be a free act, Jesus did not force his love on anyone. Neither, of course, was Jesus indifferent to the response to his offer of love.

People truly in love with another have a sense of pursuit, a holy impatience to bond with the other. Jesus asks our permission to let him love us, but he never takes a no for a final answer as long as we are alive.

His ceremonies of approach are firm, yet never intrusive. He stands outside the door of our hearts and knocks. He will neither break the door down nor leave the premises. The key to that door is inside our hearts. Jesus honors our freedom to say no. Jesus respects our human dignity enough to allow us to be participants in our destiny. He tries to show us that he is the actual source of our human dignity and can enable our humanness to achieve its full potential by his love.

Only faith can perceive these teachings of Christ's Passion. A faith that opens us to the mysticism of the Passion discovers how the various wounds of Jesus become the sources of healing for a person. It is perhaps easier for some of us to identify with the interior drama of Christ as wounded healer. But Jesus was not an angel. He had a body. Clearly his body ought not to be separated from his interior life, just as we cannot say that his interior life floats above the earth detached from his body.

The total Christ is the total witness to the process of the Passion. Jesus had taught in his Sermon on the Mount that people are blessed when they are persecuted and abused for the sake of the kingdom. He witnessed that in the scourging and crowning which prompted his thirst.

Just as his soul cry of abandonment awakens us to the desolation of his spirit, so also do the body-cries of thirst and pain remind us of the totality of his cross. Christ asks each of us to draw what we can from the full tapestry of his witness, depending on where we find ourselves in relation to him. In a multitude of ways he keeps saying to us: "Let me love you."

For Reflection

1) Jesus used his physical thirst as an occasion to express his spiritual desire to have a love relationship with us. He is basically saying, "Let me love you." Do you as a matter of course think of Jesus as someone who wants to love you? How have you responded? Do you have difficulty in letting anybody love you, let alone Jesus? Why? Do you like to be loved, but dislike returning love?

2) The physical sufferings of Christ occasioned his physical thirst. His spiritual goals caused his spiritual thirst for souls. How often does it occur to you how much love other people need? Do you tire of the thought of loving others? What good experiences have you had in showing love to others?

Prayer

Jesus,

your thirst to love me
makes me think of how I have reacted
to your overtures of love.
I wonder why I pull back from your love
even when I know how beneficial it is.

I am grateful that you never leave the door of my heart
even when I am stubborn about opening it.
Send your Spirit's guiding hand to take my own
so that I may throw open the door of my heart
to the best love I shall ever know—yours.

Amen.

THE SIXTH WORD

The Silence of the Lamb

It is finished.   JOHN 19:30b

Jesus knew that his hour had come to pass from this world to the Father. He who loved all people in the world and loved them to the very end had finished proving his love on earth. At Easter Jesus would prove it forever in his glorified presence. Jesus had finished the earthly manifestation of his love that, in biblical terms, was one continuous act of worship.

Jesus grew up in a biblical world where rich forms of worship developed from Abraham's time to his own. His community of believers meditated on the first creation story and concluded that God had called them to participate in the loving care of the earth and its possibilities. They gazed at the rainbows and remembered the Noah story that taught them God wanted a peaceful and loving relationship between people and himself. When they made pilgrimages to Mount Zion in Jerusalem, they heard again of Mount Sinai and the gift of love and forgiveness pledged to them by God in the covenant. They celebrated these fundamental teachings in a variety of rituals, at the heart of which were five forms of sacrifice: holocaust, libation, bread-offering, friendship meal and sin-offering.

A Tapestry of Affection

Throughout his life, Jesus participated in these sacrificial acts; they undergirded his life and teachings. At Skull Hill he put finishing touches on each of them as he lived them to the full by loving us to the end. That is what he meant when he said, "It is finished." He took each form of sacrifice and wove it into a single hymn of praise and love—a tapestry of affection.

A *holocaust* transformed the offering in a fire to lift it up to God. The rising of the smoke from the altar of holocausts in front of the Temple symbolized the ascension of the offering to the heart of God. When Noah left the ark, his first act was to offer a holocaust. The fire burned into the fat of the lamb and caused a sweet smoke to rise to the heavens. Noah imagined, in an anthropomorphic way, that God smelled the aroma of the lamb (see Genesis 8:21) and was moved to bless the patriarch not just for the physical gift but also for the faith that ascended to heaven along with it.

The holocaust expressed the fundamental and absolute human dependence on God. It spoke of total and undivided loyalty to the Lord and proclaimed divine lordship over the earth. "Lifting up" was the action of the holocaust. John's Gospel frequently uses this image of "lifting up" to describe both the lifting up of Christ on the cross and his further lifting up to glory. Jesus considered his life a holocaust of obedience to his Father's will. The transforming fire of the cross would result in the Resurrection and the Father's total acceptance of Jesus.

Genesis 14 describes a *libation* or wine-pouring ceremony. Having won a victory over some neighboring enemies, Abraham and a small detachment of soldiers exultantly marched back home after the skirmish. The narrative says that a priest named Melchizedek intercepted the joyful band at King's Valley. Hearing their happy news, the priest blessed Abraham and his companions in a libation sacrifice or wine-pouring ceremony.

He took a jar of wine and poured it out over a sacred stone. Giving the wine to a sacred stone was a ritual way of putting a cup of wine in God's hands. This act symbolized their joyful thanksgiving to God for their good fortune, somewhat like toasting God for his generosity. An overflowing cup of wine was a longstanding image of an abundant grape harvest. The libation of wine, customary at grape harvests, expressed the people's gratitude for God's generosity to them.

At Cana Jesus turned water in huge jars into a river of wine. By this act he taught that his loving presence was a cause of joy. He also indicated indirectly that he would pour out the wine of his life for others, generously and without dismay. With the sixth word, we are at the moment in the Passion when Jesus finishes pouring out his life for the cause of love.

In imitation of Jesus, St. Paul spoke of his own forthcoming death in terms of wine-pouring:

> For I am already being poured out like a libation, and the time of my departure is at hand. I have competed well. I have finished the race. I have kept the faith.
> (2 Timothy 4:6-7)

Like an athlete who delights in the expenditure of strength and energy, Paul had no regrets about pouring out his life for the cause of the gospel. The memory of it caused him great joy and satisfaction. Jesus, too, finished his libation with that happy awareness that he had held nothing back when it came to loving people. He was ready to release himself for the next life.

The *bread-offering* was part of Temple worship. Twelve wheat loaves were placed on a gold table in the Temple every seven days. Incense burned in front of the loaves. The rising aromatic smoke symbolized the offering of the bread to God. At the end of the week, the priests consumed the bread and put out fresh loaves.

At the wheat harvest the high priest placed a loaf of fresh bread on the altar. He waved sheaves of newly harvested wheat over the altar and the bread, symbolically sending the first wheat to God's table in heaven. The ceremonial burning of the bread loaf, which followed, had the same meaning.

In his Bread of Life sermon at Capernaum (John 6), Jesus

identified himself as the Living Bread. That Bread would be his flesh given for the kingdom-life of people. Satan had tempted him to turn stones into bread. He refused because he was not worried at that moment about physical nourishment, but only about his goal of providing the spiritual food of God's Word for people. Finally he would turn his own body into the Bread of the Eucharist, the food for people's growth in grace.

On the cross he made a bread-offering of his broken body in witness to the futility of salvation by human effort and the achievement of salvation by divine love. As the soldiers raised his body to the cross their action was like the wave offering of wheat, reminiscent of the harvest feast. As death-inflicting pain engulfed him, he seemed like the loaf of sacrificial bread burnt and transformed into a new reality. On the cross, Jesus' body of death was becoming the Bread of Life.

The Passover supper is a *friendship meal*. Begun before the Temple was built, the Passover was mainly a domestic ceremony—a characteristic it has never lost. No priest or altar was needed for this occasion. The father of the home officiated at the ceremony. The rite began at the threshold of the tent.

The doorway marked the separation of the space protected by God from the ground threatened by the force of evil spirits. That is why ceremonies of approach to thresholds were common. Bowing, prostration, kissing the ground and touching the doorposts with sacrificial blood were variations of this custom.

For this reason Passover rites began at the tent door. The father slew a young lamb. He smeared some of the blood against the doorpost. This served as a taboo against any approaching evil spirits—such as the avenging angel in Egypt. The meat was then roasted and served at the sacred meal. Unleavened bread and bitter (wild, not cultivated) herbs accompanied the meat. Jesus' people held this feast in the month of Nisan (March-April). They chose the night of the full spring moon for the simple reason that it was the brightest night of the month and ate the meal at night by the light of the moon.

Popular biblical religion thought of this banquet as the "friendship meal." The participants were required to settle grudges beforehand and renew the bonds of friendship. Some people called this meal the peace offering as they greeted one another with the Hebrew *shalom*, "peace." Often they sent out the youngest child to find hungry strangers and bring them in for the feast. This was family worship in its most intimate and appealing form.

The Last Supper appears to have been such a meal. Jesus delivered to his apostles a homily on friendship. "I no longer call you slaves....I have called you friends..."(John 15:15a,c). The early Christians incorporated these themes of friendship and peace into their Eucharists. Jesus demonstrated friendship and peace in his hours on the cross. He forgave his enemies and reached out in friendship to the repentant thief. He became himself the ultimate peace offering, reconciling all people with God. By the death of his body and the shedding of his blood he realized the Sacrament of the Eucharist, the friendship-sacrificial meal celebrated at the Last Supper and continuing to this day.

The final form of Jewish sacrifice was the *sin-offering*. Every year, our Jewish sisters and brothers celebrate *Yom Kippur*, the Day of Atonement. These "high holy days" derived from an old purification ritual in which people symbolically shed their selfishness and sins. They confessed their sins and ritually placed them on a goat (the scapegoat), which they then drove out into the wilderness. The experience made the people feel they were again at one with God.

In the case of the crucifixion people did not heap their sins on Jesus. Rather, he willingly took them upon himself. Jesus made Good Friday the Christian day of atonement, at-one-ment, establishing forever the possibility of our unity with God. The Letter to the Hebrews explains at length that the blood of an animal could never really heal our souls, only the loving sacrifice of the Son of God, Jesus Christ.

Jesus adopted, transformed and perfected five forms of reconciling love from the five types of biblical sacrifice:

1) His obedience was the holocaust of absolute submission to his Father's will.

2) The outpouring of the wine of his life was the libation he offered for us out of love.

3) The process of death occasioned his becoming the living bread-offering for us that appears in the Eucharistic sacrament of love.

4) By witnessing nothing but peace and forgiveness throughout his entire life, Jesus became the peace offering that restored our friendship with God.

5) By taking into his heart the sin and guilt of the world and going with that into his death, Jesus created the atonement, the supreme act of reconciliation that makes it possible for all of us to be at one with God.

Eat the Bread, Drink the Cup

The Eucharistic celebration makes present, by the will of Christ, his sacrificial and redemptive act at the cross. Paul told the Corinthians that every time they ate the Bread and drank the Cup they announced the death of the Lord until he comes again (see 1 Corinthians 11:26). Many believe that the original recitals at the early Christian Eucharists were sections from the Passion.

The Eucharist encompasses the five forms of biblical sacrifice that Jesus knitted into one single hymn of praise and love to accomplish the redemption. Holocaust, libation, bread offering, friendship meal and atonement all form a seamless gestalt, an integrated unity in the Eucharistic sacrifice. Jesus brings the grace-filled power of all five types of sacrifice to bear in each Eucharistic gathering. By his creative love, he enables us to interiorize them into our spiritual lives. With varying degrees of success we try to make our lives offerings of sacrificial love that embrace the following challenges:

—We learn to make a holocaust of obedience to the will of God.

—We hold nothing back in our determination to pour out our lives in a libation of love for God and others.

—We allow the bread of our sinful selves to be broken so that space for the Holy Spirit becomes possible in our hearts.

—We witness personally the peace and friendship that we pray over, celebrate and experience.

—We unite our personal pain with that of Jesus so that we may ennoble it in the cause of atonement and universal reconciliation.

At Eucharist, therefore, we not only remember Good Friday, we also experience its sacrificial reality made present again by the power of the Spirit sent to us by the risen Christ. We have the joy of experiencing Easter as well each time we eat the Bread and drink the Cup.

Kalah

As the ninth hour approached, the sacrifice of the Passover lambs in the temple came to its conclusion. Many people find it hard to kill a lamb, because the lamb just stands there, looking right at you. The lamb does not run, does not cry out. This is the silence of the lamb. As the high priest killed the last lamb of the Passover, he uttered a Hebrew word: *kalah*, "It is finished."

At that same moment Jesus, the Lamb of God, who could barely see the Temple from where he was, said, "*Kalah*, it is finished." He bowed his head and rested it on the cross. Scripture commentator William Barclay maintains that

John's word for this action is similar to the term that describes resting one's head on a pillow and going to sleep. A great silence enfolded this moment, the silence of the Lamb of God.

Scripture teaches that the profoundest moments of the incarnation and redemption occurred in a divine silence. At his birth the almighty Word of God became flesh in the silence of the night. His passion and death recalled the words of the ancient prophet: "Like a lamb led to slaughter...,/he was silent and opened not his mouth" (Isaiah 53:7). The silence of the Lamb follows the noise of the Passion.

Revelation in its deepest expression stimulates an awe so full of wonder that only silence can best witness what has happened. The Book of Revelation teaches that there will be another divine silence at the Last Judgment. It pictures the Lamb of God opening the seven seals that release the various events associated with the final judgment. When the Lamb opens the seventh seal half an hour of silence falls over the heavens while an eagle floats in the skies, signaling the ultimate victory over evil (see Revelation 8:1, 13).

The Wondrous Cross

During Pope John Paul II's second pastoral visit to the United States, he met with leaders of other denominations in Columbia, South Carolina. Fifty thousand Christians of various denominations attended an ecumenical prayer service held in the state university football stadium.

When John Paul arrived at the stadium, the people began to sing the hymn, "When I Survey the Wondrous Cross." The stage was in one end zone. From one side of the other end zone five men appeared carrying a huge cross horizontally. From the other side, parallel to them, came five other men bearing a huge tapestry with the image of the slain and risen Lamb. They arrived at the staging area just as the last verse of the hymn was being sung, raised high the cross and the banner of the risen Lamb and planted them in the earth.

The scene evoked the *triumph* of the cross, not so evident on the first Good Friday (except to a few whose faith could penetrate the mystery), but abundantly clear on that warm afternoon in the Carolinas. Jesus had joyfully—even triumphantly—cried out, "It is finished!" His words sounded like an ending, but really they signaled a beginning.

John's Gospel describes the last breath of Jesus in terms of giving up his spirit: "And bowing his head, he handed over his spirit" (John 19:30b). The biblical word for "breath" also means "wind" and "spirit." God's breath in Scripture initiates order, creativity and new life. Genesis 1 raises the curtain on a dark, chaotic mass of water. God broods over this formless waste, breathes upon it and begins the process of creation.

Ezekiel 37 tells of a valley strewn with dry bones. God tells Ezekiel to pray over the bones. Ezekiel follows God's instruction and sees the bodies reassembled before his eyes. The revival process, however, is incomplete. The bodies still need human life. God asks Ezekiel to pray again, this time for God's life-giving breath. The breath comes; the bodies come to life, stand up and form again an army. God then explains to Ezekiel that this experience symbolizes the spiritual crisis of the chosen people. Exiled in Babylon, they feel dehumanized, lost and without hope. Their bones feel dried up and their souls prone to despair. Can anyone liberate them from their oppression and depression. Who can bring about the resurrection of a people?

While Ezekiel stands marveling at the miracle in the valley, God tells him that the liberation of the people is about to occur, caused by God's breath-spirit:

> ...I will open your graves and have you rise from them,
> O my people! I will put my spirit in you that you may
> live, and I will settle you upon your land....
> (Ezekiel 37:13b-14a)

John says that the last breath of Jesus on the cross was a giving of his spirit. In a way he seems to be saying that Jesus gave his Holy Spirit to those faithful ones who stood by the cross: his mother, who symbolizes the Church, and his beloved disciple, who stands for the Christian. At the Feast of Tabernacles Jesus had said he would give the living waters of the Spirit to those who believed in him when he was glorified (see John 7:38-39). The lifting up of Jesus on the cross was also a lifting up to glory.

Hence this last breath of Jesus signals the dawn of his gift of the Spirit. In John's Gospel Jesus gives his Spirit on Easter night when he appears to the apostles and breathes on them. Christ's final breath, therefore, both announced his human death and at the same time his divine determination that his every act—even his last one—be creative and life-giving. Just as God's breath brought life out of the chaotic waters of Genesis, so Christ's breath brings spiritual life and hope for all humans out of the chaotic waters of his death.

That breath is another form of the silence of the Lamb, for the proper environment of creativity is an island of quiet. The divine silence of Genesis accompanied the beginning of the creation of the world before any divine words were heard. The silence of the Lamb at the cross echoes that same creative solitude; it announces and produces the new creation.

For Reflection

1) When Jesus said, "It is finished," he used a liturgical text so that we would understand his saving act was an act of sacrificial love. He integrated the five forms of biblical sacrifice in his sacrifice at the cross. When you are at Eucharist, how do you renew your commitment to a love that is sacrificial? How do you take the attitudes of friendship and peace, celebrated at Eucharist, into daily life? How have you adopted the atonement/reconciliation aspect of Eucharist in your relationships with family, friends, coworkers, strangers?

2) Christ's words and deeds remain perennially inspiring and motivating. His silences—including the silence of the Lamb—evoke a similar power. Are you able to find quiet time each day? Do you want to? Do you find that meditative silence leads you to Christ? Have you discovered the creative uses of silence? Do you see a link between silence and spiritual strength?

Prayer

Jesus,

you united the diverse strands of biblical sacrifice
and made them into one act of worship at the cross.
You made each type contribute
to your total act of salvation.
You even adopted the silence of the lamb—
no verbal protests—
in the face of your executioners.
I know I need to have a sacrificial character in my love.
I could also do with more silence in my life.
Lead me to sacrificial love and creative silence.

Amen.

'There Is Bread
Beneath the Snow'

..."*Father, into your hands I commend my spirit...*" LUKE 23:46b

In biblical times Jewish mothers taught their children Psalm 31 as a night prayer: "Into your hands I commend my spirit" (Psalm 31:6a). In the Lucan account, Jesus took the night prayer his mother Mary taught him and used it for his last word, his night-of-death prayer. Having completed his earthly ministry, he then peacefully surrendered himself to his Father. In Elisabeth Kubler-Ross's stages of dying (see p. 18), acceptance is the last phase. That is apparent in Christ's last word.

Jesus has experienced a full human life and has now undergone the process of dying. He has felt the deterioration of his body and the cold fear of the approaching end. Along with every other human being's, his heart's instincts reject any idea of total destruction or obliteration of his person.

While we are alive, we can only experience dying. We do not experience death itself, except as it happens to someone else. Philosophy calls death the "terminal event." When we die, each one of us dies alone. What we do experience is the fear that there might be a permanent end once and for all. Our response to this is the irrepressible feeling that life after life is possible. Religion names that instinct the "seed of eternity" that God planted in our hearts.

Philosophy echoes this by saying that being is good, that being is better than nonbeing. The real answer to Hamlet's question is that it *is* better to be than not to be. Faith opens us to conviction and confirms it. More than anything else, love moves us to affirm the seed of eternity.

Christ knew human loneliness and fear of dying. He said so at Gethsemane and again in his cry of abandonment from the cross. Jesus was able to feel the lostness of people caught in the process of dying. Thousands of people die every hour, even as thousands more are born. But whether we think of the infant or the centenarian, we affirm that we all bear within us the fear that we shall be wiped out as persons.

Over against the biological reality of death and the dissolution of the body is the seed of eternity that rebels against death. Within every human person is the mystery of yet a new life given to us by Christ. With joy believers sing the words of the Nicene Creed, "We look for the resurrection of the dead and the life of the world to come."

> For the trumpet will sound, the dead will be raised
> incorruptible, and we shall be changed. For that which
> is corruptible must clothe itself with incorruptibility,
> and that which is mortal must clothe itself with
> immortality. (1 Corinthians 15:52b-53)

We linger these days on the personal aspects of death and dying. Though we may not be able to choose our death, we can choose our way of life, and that is a way of choosing what kind of death we will have. Our death ratifies the kind of life we have lived and the choices we have made. If we have lived with love that is how we will die. If we have indulged in hatred, lust and greed, then our deaths will ratify that kind of living.

In his seventh word, Jesus calmly and lovingly gave his life to God. Jesus could do that because that is what he always did throughout his life. He sensed as thoroughly as any human being ever will the seed of eternity; he gathered his whole being in expectation of life after life. In the poet Dylan Thomas's imagery about dying, Jesus "raged against the dying of the light" in the sense that he rebelled against death as the end of everything. But then he went "gentle into that good night" because beyond it is the warmth of love beyond all telling and the light that will never be extinguished. The peacefulness of his seventh word is the biblical *shalom*, the perfect reconciliation with God that is the model and cause of such peace for every human being.

Immediately following Christ's prayer of surrender and his death, several "prodigies" are reported by the Gospel writers: the piercing of Christ's side, the rending of the Temple veil and the resurrection of the just. These events frame the purposes of the cross and herald its basic redemptive results.

The Piercing of Christ's Side

Roman law said that the body of the executed should remain on the cross until dead. Normally it took a crucified person about a week to die but, because Jesus had been beaten so severely prior to crucifixion, he died quickly. Roman law also stated that the body of the crucified should not be buried because its dreadful witness deterred people from committing similar crimes. Birds and dogs normally consumed the bodies.

On the other hand, Jewish law insisted the body should be buried before nightfall (Deuteronomy 21:22-23). The Roman governor acceded to Jewish sensibilities on this matter during the Passover. Romans and Jews agreed that at Passover a coup-de-grace should be given to the suffering prisoners. On Good Friday, the soldiers used a mallet to break the legs of the thieves, reducing their ability to lift themselves up to breathe and thus accelerating their asphyxiation.

Jesus was already dead. The soldiers did not break his bones. Because Christ's bones were not broken, he is more firmly identified with the Passover lamb, whose bones should be left intact (see Exodus 12:46). Medieval art portrayed John the Baptist alongside of John the Evangelist in the scene of the piercing, thus adding the Baptist's witness that nothing was done to harm the Christ-Lamb's bones.

Just to be sure he was dead, a soldier plunged a lance into Christ's heart. Immediately, blood and water flowed from Christ's side. For John the Evangelist and the Christian community the event was a sign of the birth of the Church. The Church is born on the cross as the water of Baptism and the blood of the Eucharist flow from Christ's side.

The Rending of the Temple Veil

The Temple was 180 feet long, 90 feet wide and as high as a nine-story structure. The floors were covered with cypress wood and the walls carved with flowers, palm trees and angels. Small windows near the ceiling provided light for the sanctuary (see 1 Kings 6:4-31). Midway down the aisle stood the table for the 12 loaves of bread. Behind that one could see the altar of incense. Past the table and the altar, steps led up to the most sacred place in the Hebrew world, the windowless Holy of Holies, entered just once a year by the high priest. The darkness of the chamber signified the mystery of God (see 1 Kings 8:12). A veil, something like a massive tapestry, separated the Holy of Holies from the rest of the space.

When Jesus died, this "veil of the sanctuary was torn in two from top to bottom" (Mark 16:38). Poetically, one might see in this an act of mourning, typified by tearing one's garments. This "garment of God" rips apart at the death of God's Son.

Theologically, the opening of the veil for all to see would mean that God's presence, once reserved only to the high priest, was now available to all onlookers. The holy is no longer hidden. The New Testament, however, indicates that God's presence would not be seen in the Temple made with human hands. The piercing of the veil of the stone Temple meant the end of the first covenant and the beginning of the new.

The author of the Letter to the Hebrews argues that Jesus is the new high priest. His living, resurrected body is the new Temple (see Hebrews 9—10). The piercing of the veil of his flesh opened a new and definitive way of beholding God's presence. Jesus is simultaneously the high priest and the living embodiment of the atonement. He is now the center of healing and reconciliation for every human being.

The term *revelation* comes from a Greek word that means taking away a veil that hides what is behind it. The piercing of the veil of the Temple, symbolically matched by the opening of the veil of Christ's flesh, disclosed that the definitive revelation of God comes through Jesus Christ.

The Resurrection of the Saints

The third prodigy attending Christ's death was an earthquake in which "rocks were split, tombs were opened and the bodies of many saints who had fallen asleep were raised. And coming forth from their tombs after his resurrection, they entered the holy city and appeared to many" (Matthew 27:51b-53). Cosmic upheavals were a common biblical way of describing profound spiritual change. Folk religion thought of earthquakes as the footsteps of God walking across the earth to bring about a fresh order.

Jesus had used just such catastrophic language in his Last Judgment sermon (Matthew 24). His "end of the world" talk referred to the conclusion of the first covenant as well as to the final consummation of the world itself. The rumblings of the earth and the splitting of rocks, as well as the darkness at Calvary, are signs not just of an end, but the beginning of a new era of salvation.

Matthew notes that the resurrection of the saints occurs after the resurrection of Jesus. The scene recalls Ezekiel's vision of the dry bones (see p. 73). As time passed, vision acquired messianic meaning. A fresco found in the third-century A.D. synagogue of Dura-Europos depicts the Messiah standing on the Mount of Olives breathing on a valley of dry bones. The resurrected then march joyfully into Jerusalem. Matthew reports that, due to Christ's messianic work, the holy ones who had slept in death while waiting for redemption were raised up to eternal life. They are the first fruits of Christ's redemption.

The prodigies that come in the wake of Christ's death offer a revelation to those whose hearts are open. The centurion and his guards are affected by these prodigies and declare, "Truly, this was the Son of God!" (Matthew 27:54b). Their communal declaration of faith constitutes a choral climax to the crucifixion. The words of the psalm Jesus prayed in his fourth word now apply to the soldiers' collective cry of faith:

> All the ends of the earth
>   shall remember and turn to the LORD;
> All the families of nations
>   shall bow down before him. (Psalm 22:28)

After the Passion

Christian faith and imagination have never been restricted to the words of Scripture, but have faithfully attempted to fill in what is missing. Scripture does not describe what Mary did when the body of Jesus was removed from the cross. Michelangelo's Pieta supplies that missing segment.

The artist devoted two years of his life to carving it. To assure its authenticity he persuaded the Grand Rabbi of Rome to permit young Jewish men and women to pose for the hundreds of sketches he made so that Mary and Jesus would have true Semitic faces.

Other sculptors had carved pietas, but none with the power of Michelangelo's. He placed a grown man in a woman's lap. He portrayed none of the violence of the Passion: The nail holes in Christ's hands and feet are tiny. Bathed in tranquillity, Jesus and Mary glow with light because the marble is polished to velvet silkiness. Sleeping peacefully in his mother's arms, Jesus reveals a silent composure that in itself communicates a sense of the divine. Michelangelo produced a harmony between mother and son that spoke of God's new and harmonious relationship with the world.

Soon the mother must surrender her son's body to the tomb. Jesus had once said that it would be easier for a camel to go through the eye of a needle than for a rich man to enter the kingdom of heaven. Now two rich men come forward to arrange for the burial of Jesus. Both men had been secret disciples of Jesus.

Never heard from while Jesus was alive, Joseph of Arimathea undertakes the risky business of claiming Christ's body from the Roman governor and then donating his new tomb in the garden next to Calvary. Ever the cautious conservative during Jesus' life, unwilling to be seen with him publicly, Nicodemus finally throws caution to the wind and joins Joseph in burying Jesus. They are immediate proof of what Jesus had taught: "And when I am lifted up from the earth, I will draw everyone to myself" (John 12:32).

Joseph's tomb was carved out of a rock. Inside it was a flagstone used as a space for anointing. Behind that was a ledge, the final resting place of the body. Scripture says that Nicodemus brought 100 pounds of spices and oils to anoint Christ's body (see John 19:39). Such a quantity would usually be used only for a royal anointing. Nicodemus had shed all his fears and reservations and was at last prepared to express his love for Jesus with abandon. After the anointing, Jesus was wrapped in a shroud and laid to rest on the ledge. The traditional prayer at this moment was "Dust you are and unto dust you shall return" (see Genesis 3:19). Jesus, however, was to conquer death and transform humble dust into the glory of the resurrected body.

The Gospels report that the tomb is in a garden. Sin—and the death that resulted from it—had begun in a garden. Resurrection, the ultimate victory over both sin and death, occurred in a garden.

Fear and Love

Christ's life and ministry was a testimony to what true love is all about. His seven last words, like a second Sermon on the Mount, witness love in its various manifestations. To do so, Jesus removed paralyzing fear from religion. Jesus did not want us to be scared of God, like pagans living in terror of capricious gods. This kind of fear is the enemy of love. Fear does more to dampen affection than any other attitude. Defensive caution shrivels the soul.

One way fear works against love is by encouraging an escape into fantasy, often by means of alcohol, drugs and sex. This is not creative fantasy or productive dreaming. Substance abuse signals fear of the risk of loving and living.

At the cross the people tempted Jesus to believe that his mission as a Savior was not worth the pain and the effort. In the desert temptation, Satan had urged Jesus to throw himself down from the pinnacle of the Temple (see Matthew 4:6). At Calvary, the crowd yelled for him to come down from the cross. The escapist dream of popularity would prevent Jesus from taking the chance of loving people. But Jesus did not let fear make him an escapist.

The second anti-love aspect of fear is the apprehension about having one's heart broken. But one could ask, "How do you know if you have a heart, if it has not been broken?" Which is preferable: a cold heart that is intact and hard as a stone or a warm heart that has been broken and overflows with healing life for all who come near it? Jesus understood what a broken heart is like. Like a mother hen, he lamented that he wanted to nurture his people with an ocean of love (see Matthew 23:37-39). Rejection had broken his heart.

The lance thrust into his heart caused a flow of blood and water. Mystics from time immemorial have found spiritual inspiration from that event, not from a crude obsession with the physical details of the lance thrust but from the divine significance of the act. How perfectly that scene corresponds with the total love Jesus poured out throughout his life, death and resurrection!

The third dimension of fear is the inability to trust. Love without trust is like a picnic without sunshine. Too many people are so afraid of being taken that they have lost their capacity to give. They hold others at arm's length. Paralyzed by suspicion, they prefer the safety of isolation to the openness that permits them to trust and love.

True love recognizes what might happen and continues to trust anyway. Jesus demonstrated such trusting behavior. He let himself be taken and continued to be a lover and a giver despite all that happened.

Jesus understood that love is a hunger. This aching need in every person is often ignored. People do not starve just for bread, they also hunger for affection. The pervasiveness of human loneliness, especially in prosperous countries, testifies to this desire for love. Jesus knew how to make bread for the multitudes to satisfy a temporary hunger. He also created the Bread of Life, a sacrament of love to nourish the love-hunger of the spirit. The expressions of his love in the Passion and Resurrection become available to us in the sacraments, especially the Eucharist.

Pope John XXIII was fond of quoting an old Italian folk saying, *"C'e pane sotto la neve."* "There is bread beneath the snow." Rural wisdom remembers that the seed in the snow-covered earth will rise in the spring. The proverb is an image of death and resurrection.

Pope John applied the saying to those who are overwhelmed by the difficulties of life and unable to see beyond pain. They see the snows. They do not see the bread of love growing quietly underneath that white blanket. They feel only the cold above ground, not the heat beneath it. They want the results of love but fail to see how the cross makes it happen. They like the sunrise of Easter but are puzzled by the gloom of Good Friday. They need the illumination of faith to see the connection, to understand that the Bread of Love is slowly maturing beneath the snow.

One of Christ's best known sayings is about the need to die in order to live. "...[U]nless a grain of wheat falls to the ground and dies, it remains just a grain of wheat; but if it dies, it produces much fruit" (John 12:24). Christ's death and resurrection invites everyone to learn this essential lesson of loving and living. Save your life and you will lose it. Gain the whole world but lose your soul. The green blade rises from the buried grain. Wheat which has lain in the dark earth is the seed that will rise again.

There is no other answer to the problem and challenge of love. Christ came forth at Easter like the risen grain. Our hearts will have their winters of grief and pain. Christ's touch can bring them to life again. The fields of our hearts will at times lie beneath the winter snows. Love will make them rise with Christ.

The mourners laid Jesus in the grave. As they viewed him in the sleep of death, they did not think he would rise again. They laid him in the ground of the tomb like a piece of grain that would unfold and grow in silence. Yet Love would rise again like the wheat that rises green.

With the sun's love, the wheat arises green. With the Son's love, our hearts will rise again.

For Reflection

1) Christ's Passion is an act of salvation from sin and also a lesson in the art of dying. His peaceful surrender to his Father shows us the goal of acceptance we journey toward in our death process. If you have had experiences of dying people, have you seen acceptance and hope in them? What other attitudes have you found?

2) Many say that we are a death-denying people. Is that your experience? Are you that way? Do you think Jesus should have chosen another way to save us—not a violent and shameful death?

3) The imagery of the grain of wheat that must be buried and die in order to become the sheaf of wheat is a central metaphor for Christ's Passion and Resurrection. If you are to "die," what are you supposed to die to? Are you

convinced you should surrender to this "dying"? What would you prefer to do?

Prayer

Jesus,

there is no way that I can adequately thank you
for your personal love for me.
You said that the greatest love a person can show
is to die for love of another.
I have your example before me.
I know what you taught.
I see your irresistible witness.
Still, I sometimes hesitate to believe and to act.
I need momentum to go forward
with the business of Christian living.
Give me your love;
attract me in spite of my wandering purposes.
I know you are right.
I am ready to love—with a little help from you.

Amen.